How To Create A Passive Income From Your Home

Become Your Own Boss, Create Wealth And Change Your Life

Kenneth C. Lorenz

Table of Contents

Introduction 7
What to Expect From This Book?............................7
Chapter 1: Things to Know Before You Begin 9
What is Passive Income? 9
The Benefits of Making Extra Money Online.........10
The Difference Between a Traditional Job and an Online, Passive Income Source 11
The Benefits of Passive Income 11
Challenges You May Face 12
Chapter 2: Dropshipping and E-Commerce .. 15
What is Dropshipping?..15
Other Examples of E-Commerce Income Sources. 17
Print On Demand...18
How to Use These Methods to Make Quick Money 20
What Costs Are Associated? 21
How Much Money Can You Expect to Make? 21
Chapter 3: Content Writing and Self-Publishing... 23
What is Content Writing?...................................... 23
How to Make Quick Money Online Through Content Writing 24
What is Self-Publishing? 25

E-Book Self-Publishing.. 26

Amazon Kindle Direct Publishing (KDP).............. 27

How Much Money Can You Expect to Make? 28

Chapter 4: Online Advertising Income 30

Social Media Income for Your Business................. 31

Social Media Management 32

Crowdfunding Income 34

Chapter 5: Trading, Investing, and Cryptocurrency 37

The Benefits 37

Trading vs. Investing 38

The Basics of Trading and Investing 39

Types of Trading That you Can Pursue 40

Investment Options 41

Income Potential.. 45

Risk 46

What is Cryptocurrency? 47

How to Make Money Using Cryptocurrency 48

Chapter 6: Income Using Amazon 49

What is Amazon FBA? 49

How to Use It to Make Income 50

Resources You Need to Begin 50

Costs Associated 51

Profit Potential..51

Chapter 7: Online Freelance Jobs 53
  Online Consulting Platforms 53
  Online Freelance Jobs 60
  Online Freelance Platforms 61
  Editing and Proofreading 64
  Temporary Side Gigs 64
  Chores 68
  Cleaning 68

Chapter 8: Property Rentals 75
  Long-Term Rentals 75
  Short-Term Rentals 76
  Rental Property Income Potential 77
  Buying and Selling Property 78
  Tips for Investing in Income Properties 78
  How to Choose a Property Type 80
  Which Kind of Property Can Make the Most Income?
  81
  Benefits of Property Income 83
  Notes for Success 83

Chapter 9: Online Teaching and Coaching ... 86
  Tutoring Platforms 86
  Language Instruction 89
  Online Course Creation and Instruction 90
  Lessons 93

Online Coaching 94

Corporate/ Career Coaching 96

Financial Coaching 97

Translation 103

Personal Trainer 104

Chapter 10: How to Choose Which Income Source to Pursue 105

Considerations to Make Before Choosing 105

Take Stock of Your Resources 106

Tips for Success 109

How to Balance Online Income and Your Day Job 113

How to Transition From Your Day Job to Full-Time Online Income 115

Chapter 11: Starting your Own Business 119

Examples of Quick, Profitable Online Businesses 119

Car Rental Businesses 119

Starting Your Own Car Rental Business 122

Food Delivery Businesses 123

Dog Walking 124

House Sitting 125

Conclusion 127

Introduction

These days, anyone who has an internet connection and a computer or smartphone can begin making money fast. This is one of the wonderful things about this futuristic world we live in. With these tools, you can become your own boss and begin making an income from the comfort of your home. This book will teach you how to do this and set you up for success from the start!

This book will teach you everything you need to know and help you prevent making mistakes along the way. Take it from someone who has done it and who is somewhat of an expert in the field; making quick money is possible, and it's easier than you think!

What to Expect From This Book?

Throughout this book, I will teach you all the information and skills you need to begin making quick money! I will also teach you how to become a successful entrepreneur.

I will begin by teaching you about *passive income,* and you will learn about how this can be the key to financial freedom.

This book aims to help you create extra streams of income for yourself and turn them into consistent, growing income. The goal is to set you up so that you can eventually make enough money to make large, secure investments like purchasing a house or investing in stocks!

Throughout this book, you will find a plethora of examples of different methods for making quick money, as well as various business ideas that can provide you with passive income. This information will help you understand the difference between a part-time job and a side hustle and help you begin making passive income for yourself!

Continue reading if you want to find freedom from your day job and be your own boss! This book will help you develop a passive income source for yourself. It's never too late to begin saving for retirement or your next vacation! It's never too late to get out of debt once and for all!

Chapter 1: Things to Know Before You Begin

We will begin the book by defining several terms so that you can continue reading the following chapters with confidence! This chapter will teach you about passive income, online income, and the many benefits that come with them.

What is Passive Income?

Before we dive into the rest of this book, wherein we will discuss specific examples of ways to make quick money, I will begin by defining the term *passive income* for you.

Passive income is a type of income derived from a business or enterprise in which you are not actively involved.

On the other hand, *active income* is income paid to you in exchange for a series of services that you have performed. Examples of active income include; salaries, wages, commissions, tips, and business endeavors. Examples of this kind of income would be working as a teller at a bank. In this type of position, you would be paid in salary or hourly. You would be getting paid in exchange for the services you perform for that bank's daily operations. Another example would be a waiter working at a restaurant; their wages per hour are their active income, as are the tips they make. They actively perform services for one specific establishment and are an employee of the business.

As I mentioned, passive income is a type of income that comes from a business or enterprise where the person is not actively involved. Passive income may include income from a rental property, a company you have shares in, or renting out your car on share websites. Passive income is different from the types of jobs people usually spend their time on because passive income does not require nearly as many hours.

The Benefits of Making Extra Money Online

The best way to make extra money to supplement your salary is by getting yourself a *side hustle*. A side hustle is almost like a 'second-job' that provides you with another source of income. Rather than being employed by someone else or another company, a side hustle is a business that you opened yourself 'on the side' that is either your passion project or another method to help make you money.

With financial security becoming a considerable problem for nearly 50% of Americans, side hustles have become a popular option for people looking to get out of debt or are just interested in starting their own business.

The Difference Between a Traditional Job and an Online, Passive Income Source

You might be wondering why it matters which type of income you make when they both produce money for you in the end? Well, it matters because your ability to accomplish your financial goals depends on you understanding these two different terms.

In the simplest terms, active income (from a traditional job) means that you are physically doing something to obtain income. In contrast, passive income means you are 100% hands-off or close to it. Side hustles are not the same as a second job or a part-time job. Your employer will be managing your time and how much pay you receive for that time at a part-time job. On the other hand, side hustles give you the freedom to decide how much you want to earn and how many hours you want to work.

The Benefits of Passive Income

If you want to make enough money to help you save for your retirement or make investments, your day job salary may not be enough. The ideal situation is to provide yourself with a second income source that does not take up much of your time. This will speed up the process of achieving your life goals and will mean that you still have time to spend with your family or on the other areas of your life that require attention.

Challenges You May Face

While making extra income comes with many benefits, it will also come with some challenges. These challenges do not need to discourage you; instead, they can motivate you. It is important to understand the challenges you may face before they arise to be prepared to overcome them and bounce back.

It will require a lot of time and energy at the beginning.
You will build your side hustle during the hours outside of your day job as you get started. Due to this, your working hours for your side hustle will likely take place during weekends, evenings, or holidays.

The reason for this is because side hustles may not generate enough (or any) income until you get the proper traction and marketing to begin making money. Having a full-time job enables you to have the ability to pay your bills while also spending some of your free time building your side-hustle, so eventually, it does start creating a separate stream of income.

This will likely be an adjustment initially, but once you establish your side hustle of business, you will begin to see that you have more money and more time than ever before.

Employ the Right Mindset
Mindset is crucial when it comes to financial success and making quick money. The way you think and feel about money has everything to do with how you spend

it and save it. People with negative mindsets towards money such as; "I never have enough of it anyway, might as well buy this new television now" or "If I don't spend it on something I like, the money will go elsewhere." Mindsets like this cause your finances to always get you stuck in a vicious cycle. Financially intelligent people typically have strong self-discipline. In many cases, self-discipline is the key to financial success.

Many researchers suggest that the most critical thing in a person's ability to become financially successful is their self-discipline level. Self-discipline is responsible for helping people stay focused on reaching their goals, giving them the grit that they need to stick with difficult tasks, and overcoming barriers and discomforts as they push themselves to achieve greater things. Let's refresh our memory on the definition of self-discipline. Self-discipline is the ability of a person to control their impulses, reactions, behaviors, and emotions. It allows them to let go of instant gratification in exchange for long-term gain and satisfaction. It's the act of saying no when you want to say yes. Self-discipline isn't about living a restrictive and boring life without any enjoyment. It's almost impossible to be 100% self-disciplined in every single area of your life. Rather than trying to be disciplined at everything you do, you can use it to focus on the most important things.

As you begin your journey to creating your side hustle, it is important to recognize that you will likely face some obstacles. By accepting this fact before they arise, you will not be surprised, but rather you will feel prepared.

Before you begin, take some time to write in your journal about what some possible obstacles may be. Once you have done this, take some time to plan and decide how you will deal with them when they arise so that they do not disrupt your progress or cause you to resort to old ways that are unhealthy.

By setting yourself up for success in this way, you will be able to tackle any challenge without having your new lifestyle jeopardized.

Chapter 2: Dropshipping and E-Commerce

Our first discussion of lucrative and quick income sources is something called *Dropshipping* and *E-Commerce*. Let's dive into the different ways that you can begin to make money using online stores.

What is Dropshipping?

Dropshipping is a relatively new business model that people can use to run lucrative online stores. Dropshipping is simple; essentially, you have your online store with items of your choice to sell. You also have a relationship with a wholesaler that can sell your products at wholesale prices.

You could sell items including watches, mugs, clothing, electronics, and anything else you can dream of. Once a customer purchases an item from your store, you will then purchase your item from the wholesaler and have the wholesaler mail that item to your customer directly. You don't have to hold any inventory in your home with Dropshipping, and you don't have to make many items from scratch.

You also benefit from not having to pre-buy inventory, so you minimize the risk of producing a loss. What I mean by this is the traditional way to run an online store is to have an inventory for things, right?

For instance, let's say you wanted to run an online watch business, and you bought ten watches for this season at the cost of $15 each. However, by the end of the season, you only sold five watches at $40 each. Selling your items in this way means that you spent $150 on your inventory and only made $200; that's $50 profit, and you are left with five watches that are now out of season.

Dropshipping allows you to minimize your risk of having leftover, unsellable product by purchasing items and selling them as the orders come in, therefore, maximizing your profit and minimizing risk. In the same example of watches, if you only had five orders for that season and bought five watches as those orders came in, you have made a $125 profit compared to the measly $50 profit.

Numerous online platforms allow you to utilize the Dropshipping method. Some examples include;

Shopify
Shopify is a very popular Dropshipping platform that is increasing in popularity each year. Shopify helps users by connecting them with suppliers who will ship the products to their customers directly.

Shopify has two options for sellers:

1. Shopify will connect you with North American or Asian suppliers who can fulfill your orders as they come in.

2. Shopify can help you by connecting you to online suppliers like AliExpress or Amazon, who can fulfill your orders for you.

With the first option, you will likely be connected with a supplier specializing in the products you are looking to sell. With the second option, you will be connected with a marketplace that carries and sells every product under the sun.

The potential is limitless when it comes to these kinds of online stores, and the best part is that you do not need to hold onto any stock to run your store!

Alibaba.com
Alibaba.com is another method for Dropshipping. Alibaba is similar to Amazon in that it sells virtually anything you can imagine for affordable prices. With Alibaba, you can sell any products that they carry to customers, and you remain virtually hands-off throughout the entire process. Alibaba will ship the order to your customer, and you collect the money while paying a cut to Alibaba.

Other Examples of E-Commerce Income Sources

We will now learn a little about online stores, how they can be great side gigs and some of their benefits.

Online stores are similar to popular e-platforms like Amazon and eBay. However, the ones that can be utilized as side-gigs are typically on a smaller scale where sellers can post items they've made or second-hand items up for sale. There are numerous amounts of online store platforms that are extremely user-friendly and can help you make money by selling your old items or hand-made items.

Print On Demand

Print On Demand (POD) E-Commerce is similar to Dropshipping, but it requires your artistic and design abilities. What POD entails is selling prints that you have designed. The products could range from your paintings, drawings, graphic design, etc. You are then selling your designs printed on items of the customers' choice like posters, phone cases, t-shirts, tapestries, and many other options. You can choose only to sell one form of a product like specifically phone cases, or you can sell your designs on any imaginable printable surface. POD is ideal for someone who has a strong artistic ability to create designs. Depending on the popularity of your art, this can be a business with extremely high earning potential.

The costs simply consist of the items you want to print on (e.g., t-shirts, phone cases) and a company to do the actual printing itself. For instance, if a printing company agrees to print your design for $10 on a t-shirt and the t-shirt costs $5, the total cost for your t-shirt + design is $15. If you are selling those shirts for $40, you are bringing in $25 of profit. Again, the great part about this is similar to drop shipping; you only have to pay for the cost of the orders WHEN you get the orders. Paying upon order prevents you from holding a stock of different sized t-shirts with different prints, which will cost you a fortune if the business is slow. You only need to pay for costs when you get an actual order, which will guarantee your profit. Platforms that support this type of online store include Printful.com, Printify.com, and Teespring.com.

As a creative person, this side gig is highly beneficial for creating and selling tees or merchandise you create. This option is especially beneficial for those who may already pursue creative endeavors, such as if you are a musician, for example. That way, you can sell merchandise for your band.

If you already have an online platform that markets your work, it is good to add an online store to do POD business. You can sell your band logo and album covers in the form of t-shirts and other merchandise! Having multiple stores can increase your streams of passive income. That way, you still have plenty of time to pursue other side gigs to make you money.

Etsy
If you have artistic talent and have hobbies making art, running your own Etsy online store is an amazing option for you. For instance, if you have a hobby in making pottery and have gotten a lot of praise for your work, you can start your own Etsy store by selling pottery items that you have made in the past and open yourself up to commission pieces as well. Etsy is a fantastic way to make money if you are already doing

your hobby regardless if it makes you money or not. You can have fun and improve your artistic ability while making some cash.

The earning potential for this is difficult to calculate as it highly depends on how successful your sales are and how you are pricing your items. For example, let's say you like to make mugs when you are doing pottery, and you make around five mugs per week. If you sold them on Etsy for $25 each and managed to sell 4 per week, you are making around $100/week and $400/month. Again, it's not a huge amount of income if your Etsy store isn't making huge sales. Still, it's good money considering that this is your hobby, and you were going to make these items anyway.

How to Use These Methods to Make Quick Money

The first benefit that comes with using online stores as your side gig is time. You don't have to invest a lot of time into it; all you need to do to get started on most of these platforms are the following:

1. Simply make an account.
2. Begin with a few items that you'd like to sell
3. Make a post
4. Reply to the interested people.

Yes, it's that simple. However, you have to keep in mind that some items receive more attention from customers than others. For instance, Apple products or any type of decently new electronics tend to get a lot of online attention. These products do well on second-hand online platforms like Letgo, Craigslist, and eBay. If you are artistically skilled and can make homemade crafts like jewelry, pottery (mugs, vases, bowls), knits, etc., you can utilize more specialized websites like Etsy.

What Costs Are Associated?

Like any other platform that we discussed in this book, you will need to pay a cut of your profits to the businesses that help you complete your orders. For example, if you have a Shopify site that hosts your store, you will need to pay them a cut of your revenue. If you use Alibaba.com to complete your orders, you will need to pay them a cut.

For example, Shopify charges sellers 2.9% plus an additional 30 cents for each transaction that your site gets. Additionally, there is a $29 monthly fee for Shopify Basic, a $79 fee for The Shopify Plan, and a $299 fee for Advanced Shopify. Each plan comes with its own set of benefits, so you will likely choose a plan according to how well your site is doing.

How Much Money Can You Expect to Make?

Dropshipping can provide you with very quick, very easy income if you know how to gain traction on your site. Imagine that you have a Shopify store where you sell watches to customers for $40. Your wholesaler sells you watches for $15. Because of this difference in cost and sale price, you make $25 of profit for every watch. The profit that you make will depend on what you are selling and what the demand is like.

When running a business, your profit is the result of your revenue, minus your costs. So, your net profit margin, otherwise known as the "bottom line," is the revenue (in dollars) remaining once every expense and type of income is calculated. This amount will include the operational expenses, the cost of the goods you are selling, and any other expenses such as taxes, debts, and other payments. This number reflects a business's ability to generate profit from its income. This number will become important to you as you begin your business, as it will help you keep track of how well your business is doing. This number will also help you to determine when you can transition from your day job to a full-time business owner.

Before we begin the next chapter, I kindly ask that if you like this book and think that others would also enjoy the information contained within these pages, please leave us a positive review on Amazon! Your kind words will go a long way in helping us get this carefully researched information across to as many people as possible!

Chapter 3: Content Writing and Self-Publishing

Content writing and self-publishing are great ways to make money on the side, in addition to your regular day job. Let's take a look at some of these methods and how you can utilize them to make quick money. In terms of flexibility, freelance writing work is extremely flexible since you can do it anywhere and anytime. Let's begin.

What is Content Writing?

Overall, there are numerous ways that you can make money in the realm of content creation. Content creation can include anything from creating unique videos, audio, or articles to writing business pieces for companies.

The Content Writing Industry includes many different types of writing jobs, including business writing, educational article writing, and copywriting. More specifically, the content you could write includes company blogs, LinkedIn articles, product review articles, and specific niche blogs. The side jobs within this category are specialized within the business writing industry. This includes any types of company blogs, LinkedIn articles, and e-books.

How to Make Quick Money Online Through Content Writing

When it comes to side gigs in content creation, content writing is a great choice. There are a few platforms that help connect content writers to businesses and people that require this talent.

One way to generate income from writing is to start your own independent writing side gig. This method is more elaborate than utilizing platforms to connect you to clients as it requires you to find your clients and pitch your skills based on your needs. You can do this by developing a strong sales pitch that consists of your experience, writing skills, and an explanation of why you are a good candidate for the job. Businesses tend to look for people who can write articles, books, and white papers.

There is a TON of undiscovered business in this area, and all it takes to tap into a steady and high source of side gig income is finding the right client who trusts in your skills. One method to approach finding clients is looking for Content Managers or businesses on LinkedIn and reaching out to them. Try to choose businesses that you know require writers.

To generate business, it is a numbers game. The more people you reach out to with your services, the more likely you will get a hit. Do this at least 100 times a day with different businesses and positions of people; you will likely get some hits back to learn more about what you can offer. The best part about this method is that it has high earning potential if you can find yourself a handful of steady clients. However, if luck isn't on your side, this is not a steady income source as you have to spend hours reaching out to people and pitching your services, and you could end up not having much return on it. This method's flexibility is very high; as I said, you can write anywhere and anytime. The hardest part about making this side gig method work is getting the clients, to begin with.

What is Self-Publishing?

Self-publishing is a quickly emerging industry that gives people the potential to make large sums of money very quickly. Self-publishing is done when a person publishes their works by themselves without using a publishing company. In this way, publishing allows the person to maintain ownership of all profits and royalties made by their work. If your book or piece of work makes large sums of money, you do not have to pay part of your profits to the publishing company that helped you, which is why this is such an attractive income source.

With the emergence of the internet, this has become a much more accessible way to make money than it used to be since you can self-publish in an e-book or online format instead of publishing in paper format. Below, we will look at the most popular form of self-publishing material, the e-book.

E-Book Self-Publishing

There are a few different ways to make money through self-publishing, both active and passive. We will look at these methods below.

1. One great way to benefit from content writing in a passive form is by writing books or writing pieces and uploading them to various locations, which will earn you money when people pay to read them. For example, if you write an e-book, you can sell it on amazon or other e-book hosting locations. This way, your book will make money each time someone buys it, and this provides you with passive income.

2. Another way is to write e-books for an online company. That way, you get paid to write the books, but you do not have to concern yourself with the business's advertising or customer side.

3. The third way to earn extra money from E-Books is by getting other people to write your books for you and then giving them a cut of the profit when people purchase the book.

Each of these three methods has its own benefits and drawbacks, but they are all good options for making money through content writing. We will look at some of the best platforms for self-publishing in the following section.

Amazon Kindle Direct Publishing (KDP)

KDP or Kindle Direct Publishing is a section of Amazon where you can self-publish e-books. You can use this part of Amazon to either publish books that you have written or to publish books that someone has written for you, depending on which type of e-book creation source you choose to go with.

Kindle Direct Publishing is a hub where people can download e-books straight to their smartphone or Kindle e-reader. Kindle represents the future of reading books, and it has created quite a name for itself over the past ten years. KDP allows you to self-publish by getting your book out there for people across the world to see, something that would have been very difficult in the past. These days, anyone could stumble across your book, and before you know it, you could be a household name.

Amazon allows you to create an author page that contains links to your books, reviews, and a little bit of information about you. This way, if you have multiple books, people can find them all in one place. Additionally, not only can you sell e-books, but you can also sell print books from this page if your readers prefer to have a book in-hand.

Like we discussed in our Dropshipping chapter, Amazon KDP boasts a print-on-demand service, where the book will be printed when a person places the order. This presents new opportunities for income if you are a writer since you do not need to pay to have your books printed upfront, which means there are much fewer overhead costs.

How Much Money Can You Expect to Make?

Content writing side gigs require some time to ramp up as they are highly dependent on how well your content does in the marketplace. However, the profit generated from this type of work can be extremely high (we're talking over thousands per month), and therefore, people who have talent and skill in this area may be interested in this type of work.

You can always work in content writing as one of your income sources and have steadier sources that generate your income while ramping up your content. This way, you are not going without making any money, but you are still allowing yourself to generate income through creating content. Then, when your content writing picks up traction in the online marketplace, you can increase the amount of time you spend on it. The earning potential is high once you gain recognition and a name for yourself in the industry.

If you self-publish with Amazon KDP, you will keep around 70% of the profits of each book you sell. This is great when compared to authors who publish with a traditional publishing company and is one of the great benefits of self-publishing. One drawback is that if your book costs any amount over ten dollars, you will only make 35% of the profit, so keep this in mind when writing and pricing your books.

Chapter 4: Online Advertising Income

In this chapter, we will look at ways to create a side gig for yourself online by taking advantage of the world of advertising dollars! There are many ways to do this, and in this chapter, I will outline the options available to you.

Online advertising money is given to people who create content that people enjoy. This content can include videos, pictures, or anything that you can post on the internet that will get large numbers of people's attention. There is a great market for content creation advertising today since the internet and social media have such a massive presence in our society.

If you can take advantage of this, you can provide yourself with an income source by merely posting content on the internet. Once you develop a following for yourself, you can begin to make money by giving this following with pictures and videos of yourself. You will get paid through advertising and views, which is an excellent way to make passive income.

We will begin by looking at the different options you have to put your content up for everyone to see.

Social Media Income for Your Business

Social media is a relatively new way to make money since it used to be used solely to connect with friends. Still, now every business has multiple social media accounts- one on every platform. Businesses and brands use these social media accounts to reach consumers and advertise their products. These days, there are advertisements on social media news feeds so that people see them as they are scrolling through their timeline, looking at the people they follow, and product placement in the posts of people with many followers like celebrities or models.

This type of income is not just for celebrities, though; you can use this method if you are starting or running a business. You can make income by attracting new customers through social media, or you can make money with product placement deals on your business social media accounts.

There are several social media platforms, including Instagram, Facebook, Twitter, Twitch, Tumblr, and so on. All of these platforms have the potential to make you money if you have a large following, which results in lots of "likes" on your content or millions of views on your videos. The best way to maximize your following is to cross over your social media accounts, advertising one platform on the other, so that your followers can follow you on every platform possible.

With social media, the earning potential is pretty much unlimited, though you have to reach the social media celebrity level to begin earning a lot of money. If you have around 10 thousand followers, you can begin to get partnerships with brands that will give you free merchandise or up to $150. The money begins to flow when your social media following reaches one million followers. Then, you can begin to make 15 thousand US dollars for a single post! Any number of followers in between will give you some money between $150 and $15 000. A big range, I know. But it depends on the number of partnerships you have and the brands which are paying you to advertise their product for them.

In addition to having a lot of likes and views, there are some other ways that you can make money using social media. Some of these ways are outlined below.

Social Media Management

The first way we will look at is Social Media Management. Social media management is when you manage all of your social media accounts and organize what you will post to maximize your potential reach and visibility.

Hootsuite
Hootsuite is a social media management tool that you can use to manage all of your social media accounts on a single screen. You can include your Facebook, LinkedIn, Twitter, Instagram, and YouTube accounts and keep up with them from one place. In addition to monitoring your likes and views, Hootsuite allows you to schedule your posts so that you can keep your

accounts active throughout the day while you are busy or while you are on vacation away from your computer. Hootsuite also allows you to keep track of your reach and the attention your posts get and graph them so that you can compare your results over time.

There is a single place where you can view your comments, your mentions, and where you were tagged and reply straight from the Hootsuite interface. You will also receive notifications from all connected social media accounts so you can keep on top of what is going on in each of them without becoming overwhelmed by having to flip back and forth between apps on your phone.

Hootsuite works on a membership basis, so you must pay a monthly fee if you wish to use their services. This fee and more can be returned to you, however, with the money you have made on your social media platforms as they grow in popularity.

SproutSocial
Another social media management tool is SproutSocial. This social media management platform is similar to Hootsuite. It allows you to have all of your social media accounts in one place. SproutSocial has different tabs within its home page for different aspects of your social media management. It contains a tab for Publishing, where you can control your posts and schedule them, a tab for Analytics where you can track your activity, and a tab for Engagement to monitor your comments and respond to them straight from the SproutSocial page. With SproutSocial, you can link

your Facebook, Twitter, LinkedIn, Instagram, TripAdvisor, and Pinterest too.

Crowdfunding Income

Utilizing a fan base that you already have is a great way to develop a side hustle while still working on your other projects! This side gig is ideal for business owners, musicians, or artists, as you don't have to step away from your day job to make quick, extra money. This section will provide you with some examples of platforms designed to help you turn your fan base into dollars.

Patreon

The first platform we will look at is called Patreon. This platform is a way for your fans to stay connected with you and access content that they otherwise wouldn't be able to see. They can use this platform to keep up to date on your behind the scenes, your exclusive content, or your yet-to-be-released products that they want to be the first ones to access.

This platform runs on a membership basis, which means your fans will pay a monthly fee to stay connected with you. There are different membership tiers, which all include different benefits. Your fans can choose which membership tier they want to subscribe to, which informs their monthly fee.

For example, your first tier of membership can include access to a community group chat as well as a free mp3 download. Your second tier can include these things as well as access to a monthly live video chat. Deciding on your tiers and what each of them includes is up to you!

Because this platform works on a monthly membership basis, your monthly revenue will be more predictable than it would with some other types of side gigs. Fans can add specific things to their monthly fees, such as merchandise or products that you sell.

On this platform, you also have the option to include ads on your page or any other sponsorship content that you may choose, which means that you can incorporate other streams of income on your page.

Wondering how much you can earn using Patreon? Imagine your business has a social media following of 30 thousand subscribers. Out of these 30 thousand people, you could say that about 15% of those are hardcore fans or followers. The membership rates often range from $5 to $25, and the highest ones are somewhere around $100. As a result, if somewhere between 45 and 230 people are subscribers of your page on Patreon, you can hope to make between $300 and $1600 monthly, depending on the number of fans that you have engaged in your monthly plans. Patreon takes about 2.5% of the membership sales to keep its platform running.

This platform allows you to connect with your fans in a closer way, as it does not use algorithms in the same way that social media platforms do. Often, on places like Instagram, your fans may miss content from you simply because of things like what they viewed last for what they view most. With Patreon, they will never miss content from you as there is no tricky algorithm that you have to workaround.

The above methods are great ways to keep doing what you love and creating your music without sacrificing it to pay your bills. These methods are great options for people who just aren't comfortable spending more time on their side gig than their creative endeavors, as this type of side gig combines both!

Chapter 5: Trading, Investing, and Cryptocurrency

In this chapter, we will discuss the numerous ways that you can grow the money you have saved up so that it builds your wealth without much effort from you. This chapter contains a lot of valuable information, so be sure to bookmark it so that you can return to it over and over again.

The Benefits

I will begin this chapter by informing you about some of the benefits of investing and trading. Investing in a general sense is beneficial for a variety of reasons. Firstly, it allows you to grow the money you have earned much quicker than you can make it.

Imagine it would take you ten years to make $20000 in savings by putting some money from every paycheck into a savings account. Instead of making 20 thousand dollars in this way, you could invest five thousand dollars today and see it grow to 20 thousand dollars in much less time than ten years. Also, by the time you have saved $20000, the impact of inflation would mean that your 20 thousand dollars would not be able to buy you nearly as much as it would today.

This sum of money could come from your savings account, or it could be a sum of money that you make working on your side job. One great option is to take the money you make from your secondary income source and use it to invest. That way, you are still living on your day job salary and are potentially growing a large sum of money on the side.

In addition to the benefits above, investment funds can provide you with numerous other benefits, including the following:

- You can maintain control over your shares in the company or asset that you have invested in.
- The fees related to investing will be much lower when investing in investment funds than if you were to invest your money on your own.
- Your funds are managed by professionals, taking some of the work out of it for you, allowing you to rest easier than investing yourself.
- Gives you more opportunities for investing because the investment funds are shared amongst many people, allowing for more selection.

Trading vs. Investing

Trading and investing. You have likely heard of these two terms before, but do you understand the differences between them? Before we look at specific examples of investments that you can pursue, we will first learn about the differences between trading and investing.

Trading is what people do with stocks. You have likely heard of Day Traders- people who spend their days buying and trading stocks. These people aim to buy stocks at a low price and sell them at a high price, leading to profit. This can be an extremely lucrative form of income, but it comes with high risk and a requirement to understand the stock market inside and out.

On the other hand, investing involves putting money into capital and leaving that money in place for an extended period. For example, purchasing a property and holding onto it while the market value increases. This is different from trading because it does not involve the same quick buying and selling. We will look at examples of each below so that you can better understand the differences. For now, though, you must understand that neither is better than the other, only that they are two options available to you.

The Basics of Trading and Investing

To understand trading and investing, we must first understand a few technical terms. Before defining what *investment funds* are, I must define the term *capital* for you.

Capital is a term used to describe assets. In this case, these assets are of the financial type. Financial assets can include the following:

- Cash
- Funds from financing
- Funds in deposit accounts
- Securities
- Cash equivalents

Now that you understand what capital is, I will define investment funds for you. Investment funds are a type of capital that is held by many investors at the same time. These investors all maintain ownership of their shares of the capital.

Types of Trading That you Can Pursue

Now that you understand trading and investing, we will look at examples of each to give you a better idea of your options.

Stocks
Stocks are one of the most basic investment forms and likely the most common one you hear about. In the most basic explanation, stocks are securities that represent an ownership share in a company. Companies will issue stocks to raise money from the general public to grow and invest in their own business. Stocks are then exchanged in the stock market. The stock market, such as the New York Stock Exchange, is made up of exchanges. Stocks are listed on a specific exchange and allow sellers and buyers to come together to sell/buy shares of certain stocks. The exchange tracks the supply and demand, which usually directly relates to the price or each stock.

Stock prices fluctuate daily, and people who own stocks hope that stocks that they own will increase in value with time. For instance, if you bought a stock for company A for $20 apiece, and that stock grows to be worth $50 apiece in three years, you have made $30 over three years ($10 per year). However, stocks carry some of the highest risks than other investments, but they can also reap higher rewards. Some people look at stocks as a type of 'gambling' as it is difficult to predict the increase/decrease of stocks. Take a look at bitcoin; for example, what used to be a $7 stock grew to be worth $7000 per stock in the past few years. Although this may sound promising, it can happen the other way around too. You can buy a bitcoin stock for $7000 now and hope that it will grow to $14,000 or more. However, it could drop down back to $7, causing you to lose significant amounts of money.

Exchange-Traded Fund (ETF)
An ETF (exchange-traded fund) is a type of investment fund that involves several securities like stocks. This group of securities follows a common theme.

Investment Options

We will now learn about several investment options available to you today.

Bonds
Unlike a stock, a bond is a kind of loan that a company takes out, but instead of asking the bank for this

money, they ask investors for money by asking them to purchase bonds. As an exchange for the capital, the company will pay an annual interest rate on the bond, annually or semiannual, and then return the principal loan when it reaches maturity.

There are six features that you should look out for before purchasing a bond:

- **Maturity:** Maturity refers to the date when the bond is paid, and when the initial chunk of money is returned to you. Maturity is often divided up into; short-term (1 – 3 years), medium-term (10+ years), and long-term (20+ years)

- **Secured/unsecured:** This term describes the fact that a bond can either be secured or unsecured.

  A secured bond promises the bondholders certain assets in the event that the company is unable to repay the money. The term can also be described as "collateral." If the firm cannot pay back its money, then the agreed-upon asset will go to the lender.

  Unsecured bonds are the opposite. Any collateral does not back them up. These bonds will return only a small portion of the initial investment that you made if the company cannot pay back the money.

- **Liquidation Preference:** When a company declares bankruptcy, it will repay its investors following a specific order as they liquidate their assets. Senior debt is what the company will repay first, and junior debt will be paid last. Stockholders will then get the remaining money if there is any.

- **Coupon:** This term is used to describe the amount of interest that the company pays to bondholders on either an annual or semiannual basis. The Coupon can be referred to as the nominal yield or the 'coupon rate.' To calculate this, divide your annual payments by the face value of your bond.

- **Tax Status:** Most corporate bonds are included in taxable investments, but if the bonds are municipal or government bonds, they will be tax-exempt. Any income or gains will be taxed. However, tax-exempt bonds will have a lower interest rate than taxable bonds.

- **Callability:** The company can pay off some bonds before its maturity. A company sometimes wishes to "call" the bonds if the interest rate allows for better borrowing rates.

Real Estate Investment Trust (REIT)
REIT stands for Real Estate Investment Trust. A REIT is a type of business that operates, finances or owns real estate that generates income for them. REITs are modeled similarly to the way that mutual funds

operate, in that they pool capital from several different investors. This type gives investors dividends because the company can buy various real estate investments. The investor themselves does not need to buy, finance, or manage any of these properties on their own.

Typical properties in a REIT portfolio include hotels, apartment complexes, healthcare facilities, data centers, or can include telecommunications such as; fiber cables and cellphone towers. REITs also require a bit more knowledge in real-estate real estate as some REIT portfolios are a mixed bag of different properties. I don't recommend REITs for beginner investors as there are many risk factors and areas where you must learn about. However, many professional investors and traders swear by REITs, so if this is something you'd like to do, please do some heavy research and learn about the REITs in your market before investing any money.

Target-Risk Fund (TRF)
This kind of investment is a type of investment that involves a portfolio of a mix of stocks, bonds, and other types of investments. This type provides the investor with a varied mix of investments in one package.

Low-Cost Funds
Lost cost funds are an investment option for those who do not want to part with large amounts of money upfront. This kind of investment is a great option for risk-averse individuals, as these funds do not involve a person managing them, resulting in lower fees for investors.

Hedge Fund
A hedge fund is an investment company that people provide their money with to invest in. These hedge funds use the investors' money to purchase stocks or bonds while trying to beat the market or make experimental investments.

Commodities
Commodities are part of an average American's life each day. In its simplest form, a commodity includes a good that can be used in commerce to interchange with other goods in the same category. For example, grains, beef, gold, natural gas, and oil are traditional commodities.

Commodities are an important way for investors to add variety into their portfolios past the included traditional securities. Since commodity prices usually shift opposite the stocks, investors most often rely on commodities during market volatility periods. Professional traders usually do commodity trading as it is more complicated and does require quite a bit of knowledge and education to pull off effectively. For that reason, I won't go into detail about how commodities are traded and the functions.

Income Potential

With investing and trading, it is difficult to come up with a range of income potential. This is because the amount you can make depends on the amount that you invest or trade. For example, the more money you have, the more stock shares you can purchase. The more stock shares you purchase, the more money you have the potential to make if the value of those shares increases. For this reason, it is highly dependent on several factors. To get a better idea of this, I recommend speaking to a broker who can help you decide how to invest your money.

Risk

In the world of investing, things are changing by the second. There will always be a risk component involved in investing and trying to grow your wealth. There is no guarantee that you will succeed, but many people decide that the potential gain is worth the risk.

Every person who invests their money could see vastly different results from each other, depending on so many factors. You must remember that there is no "one size fits all" approach to investing. As long as you prepare yourself by learning the required information to prepare yourself, there is not much more that you can do. In the world of investing, there are no mathematical certainties, only risk, and reward.

With that being said, it is up to you to decide which risks you are willing to take and which you are not. Nobody else can decide for you, and nobody can predict the outcome. Keep this in mind as you begin investing your money. I wish you luck!

What is Cryptocurrency?

Another great way to make quick money online and one that fits into the umbrella of trading and investing is something called Cryptocurrency. You have likely heard of Bitcoin before, but do you know what it is? In this section, I will explain Cryptocurrency and how to use it to make money.

At its most basic level, Cryptocurrency is a digital form of currency. You can use this digital currency to buy things, like services or goods, and then sell them for a profit. One great way to understand Cryptocurrency is by thinking about it, like the tokens or tickets that you buy when you go to the fair or the casino. You need to pay money to buy this form of currency, which you then exchange for gameplay or a ride.

There are many different types of Cryptocurrency, Bitcoin being only one example. Other examples include *Chainlink, Ethereum,* and *Tether*.

There are also many benefits to using Cryptocurrency, namely the absence of banks controlling the money, which means that instead of decreasing in value over time (like when you keep money in a savings account), this currency can increase in value over time. Additionally, people are turning to Cryptocurrency for its digital security.

How to Make Money Using Cryptocurrency

One way to make money by using Cryptocurrency is to buy it and resell it at a higher value. This is similar to investing in a property and waiting for its value to increase before selling.

To do this, you will need to have a lump sum of money to purchase the Cryptocurrency, but once you do, you are likely to make money in the future as each currency unit's value increases.

Some people consider this to be a risky investment, so do some research and choose before you invest.

Chapter 6: Income Using Amazon

In this chapter, we will discuss how you can use Amazon to make an income. We have touched on this throughout the book so far, but we will discuss it in more detail.

Similar to Shopify, as we discussed in our Dropshipping chapter, Amazon can also provide you with a simple and easy way to sell products to customers all over the world. In addition to their Dropshipping services, Amazon also offers Amazon FBA, which we will look at below.

What is Amazon FBA?

Amazon FBA stands for "Fulfillment by Amazon." This is a service that Amazon provides to businesses who want to use their warehouses, packaging, and delivery services. For example, imagine that you are a business that sells computer parts. If you were to conduct business on your own without the help of Amazon, you would need to pay the following:

- to rent a warehouse to store your products
- purchase packing materials
- pay people to package your products when you get orders
- pay services to deliver your products to your customers.

Instead of doing this, you can use Amazon FBA, and all you need to do is send them your products to keep a stock on-hand for you. This way, your customers can put their orders in through the Amazon website, and they will receive their product the next day (if they subscribe to Amazon Prime) packaged neatly in an Amazon box.

How to Use It to Make Income

This method makes your income by eliminating the costs of storing and shipping for you. Depending on your products' size, you may require a lot of space and many shipping materials to get your products to your customers. Since Amazon is a force in terms of their packing and shipping quality and speed, allowing them to take care of it for you could save you money, thus increasing your profits.

Additionally, Amazon will take care of the customer service side of things, so you can spend your time and money focusing on other things. This way, you do not need to hire customer service representatives or spend time taking care of this yourself.

Resources You Need to Begin

To get started with Amazon FBA, you need the following resources:

- Product in-hand, ready to ship to Amazon Warehouses

- A business name and contact information
- Enough money to create more product if needed and to pay the Amazon monthly fee (if that is the plan you choose)

To get started with Amazon FBA, you don't need too much, especially since they can take their charges from your first order. This is a great option if you have a product ready to go and you have a little bit of money to start you off.

Costs Associated

There are some costs associated with using Amazon FBA, such as warehouse storage space usage and the fees that Amazon takes from each order for using their services. These fees range depending on the package that you choose.

For example, their cheapest plan will cost you 0.99 cents USD per unit of product that you sell. If you sell many units, you may instead opt for the Professional Plan, which costs $39.99 USD per month, for unlimited unit sales. Additionally, Amazon charges between 8 and 15% per item you sell as a fee for their website and advertising services (called a referral fee).

Profit Potential

Using Amazon FBA can provide you with some high income, depending on how many units you sell. For example, imagine that you sell 100 units of your product in one month. Imagine that you make $10 on each unit of your product sold. If you choose the Professional Plan, it will cost you $39.99 for the month to ship unlimited orders to your customers. If Amazon takes around 8% of your profits, this will leave you with about $885 in profit that month.

This is a rough estimate, but if you are running this business on the side, considering that it does not require much effort on your part, $885 USD of additional income is a great bonus to your day job salary.

Chapter 7: Online Freelance Jobs

This chapter will focus on secondary income sources that will allow you to use skills you may already have. Depending on which skills you have, they can prove extremely beneficial for freelance work. We will begin with consulting before moving onto freelance work.

Online Consulting Platforms

Consulting is an excellent option for people who have educated, excellent and sound advice to give others in specific areas, depending on your expertise.

Consulting can be a great side gig for those looking to have flexible hours and earn good money while still having time to do the other things they need to do in life. Depending on your background, there are different forms of consulting that you may be able to pursue. We will look at some of these below. We will also discuss specific platforms that you can use to get started if you wish to begin consulting on the side.

Clarity. FM
Clarity is an online consulting platform that connects experts with people looking to get advice on business-related topics such as Marketing, Social Media, and Entrepreneurship, among others. If you have knowledge and experience relating to these areas, you may begin making money by sharing this advice with other people! If you are naturally somewhat of an entrepreneur, you may have the skills to become an

expert with clarity. The great thing about clarity is that it has the flexibility to allow you to be an expert in a wide variety of topics within the larger umbrellas of Sales & Marketing, Technology, Skills & Management, and Product & Design. Within these umbrellas are a wide range of topics, and many people can find topics within these that they are knowledgeable in and confident giving advice in.

To begin earning money, you sign up as An Expert, and once you go through the onboarding process, you can begin having calls with people seeking your advice. You will get paid by the minute, so you are cashing in for each minute you spend on a call with a person seeking your advice. Most people charge between $2 and $7 per minute, depending on their experience, while the occasional expert will charge $50 to $80 per minute. This all depends on what type of experience and education you bring to the table. Experts set their rates, and choosing what rate to set will depend on your ability to show value. By starting somewhere around $1.60 per minute, your 30-minute call will get you $50. Based on this, you can decide what to charge. Clarity pays their experts every 15 days through PayPal, and 15% of your pay is given to the company.

The majority of people who use clarity for advice purposes are new entrepreneurs or business owners looking to filter out all of the free advice they can find online and get real expert advice fast. By doing a quick search on the platform, you can find experts ready to advise on a vast range of topics, including the music industry.

Inzite.com
Inzite.com is another consulting platform that provides its users with advice on various topics through the use of consultants who are experts in their field. On Inzite, the consultants are called Advisors, and the advice-seekers are called Users. Inzite includes a wide variety of experts, including coaches, mentors, and consultants, who can offer support in any area of expertise when combined. Like Clarity, Inzite offers advice on a wide range of topics, music being one of them as there is an entire section of their Discover page titled "Arts, Music & Culture." If you are experienced in any specific area with advice to give, this could be a great solution for your side gig.

As an Advisor on Inzite, you can set your availability to let people know when you are available for meetings. The meetings come in the form of phone calls, instant messaging, and video chats. You have the option to offer free initial information sessions or to begin with paid sessions. To become an Advisor, you simply complete an online application form through their website. You hear back once the application has been processed.

Most calls work on a fixed-price basis, as the duration of the call will be pre-determined. You can decide on your fixed prices for pre-determined call lengths (30min, 45 min, etc.), or you can set an hourly rate that the user would pay by the minute. If the call goes overtime, the user is charged your per-minute rate. Inzite does not have subscription fees for its Advisors' users, but it takes 15% of your earnings. The calls are free of charge as they happen on a conference line set up by the platform. Your funds are deposited into your account on the platform, after which you can withdraw them into your bank account free of charge.

COMATCH.com

COMATCH is a consulting platform that focuses on consulting for large companies in need of business consulting. The topics of consulting that COMATCH concerns itself with are Startup Business Solutions, Management, Information Technology, Market Research, Operations and Strategy, and Finance. To work with COMATCH, you must have some business knowledge, but you may have some of this experience if you are a musical entrepreneur.

COMATCH works with large companies that submit a business proposal outlining their project and what type of consulting they require. From here, consultants are selected based on their knowledge of and experience with the project specified. The company can then choose between the submitted consultants by interviewing them over the phone or simply deciding on the best match. A contract is signed, and the consultant can begin working on the project. The platform itself is in charge of invoicing and recording all logistics to ensure that you are paid what you are owed. Your income possibilities will vary depending on your experience and the number of projects you are selected for based on how closely your skills match the current projects. It is difficult to estimate compensation as the company must first put you through their hiring process.

COMATCH began as a company in Germany but has quickly spread worldwide, including the United States. If you have skills and experience in business and would like to put these skills to use as a freelance, remote consultant, you can do so through COMATCH. Their hiring process is a little more stringent than the others, but it comes at a good price when it is time for payday. This company employs its consultants on a full-time basis. COMATCH allows artists or any other people to pursue their art (or other endeavors) while still making enough money to live well.

Independent Business Consulting
A business consultant focuses on helping business owners assist and guide them to run their business by clarifying their company's vision and how it aligns with their personal goals.

Alternatively, business consultants can help people looking to start their own business (entrepreneurs) and help guide them to follow the best business practices and help them create a vision for what they want their business to be. In simpler words, business coaches follow a process to help grow a business from its present state to where the client wants their business to be.

An essential part of business consulting is for the consultant to help the client understand that their company's vision and story are entirely theirs to create. Business consultants don't help their clients by creating their businesses for them; instead, they help them discover their business model and plan to execute it.

A business consultant's main role is to introduce concepts, tools, and processes to their clients that help them grow their organization and team to create a good, lucrative business. Here are a few other responsibilities of a business consultant:

- Optimize the alignment of the entire organization
- Increase accountability within teams and individuals in the organization
- Strengthen the company culture
- Increase the focus of the organization
- Make better decisions regarding the 'people.'
- Develop strategies that are more effective in growing the business

A business consultant can target individual clients, group clients, or corporate clients. In most cases, business consultants aim to market their services to corporate clients, as that is where they can bill the most hours at the highest rates. However, there are still a plethora of clients that fall into the individual category. Most of the time, these are people who have already started their small to medium-sized businesses and are looking to grow them further. They could also be people that do not have their own business yet, but who wish to build their own. In both of these cases, the business consultant helps assess what the client's current state is in terms of their business and helps them plan execution to grow their business to the place they want it to be.

Depending on what type of client the business consultant has, they could deliver their sessions in-person, over the phone, or by video conferencing. Most corporate companies that hire business consultants would require them to come into their workplace to deliver these sessions. In contrast, entrepreneur type clients may deem over the phone sessions sufficient.

Business consultants typically have some sort of background or career within the specific field that they are consulting on. This can range from having run their own business before having worked in management or executive-level positions in the business field. A business consultant must have a good grasp of how businesses work and how to grow them in size, revenue, and overall vision.

Like I mentioned earlier, there isn't a specific prerequisite for any type of consulting. It is important that you can assess yourself and see where your strongest skills lie to help you determine what consulting niche makes the most sense for you. Some business consultants specialize within the entrepreneur realm only, while others will take clients that are established companies.

Online Freelance Jobs

When it comes to freelance work, there are a plethora of different types. You could do freelance work in whatever skill or profession you already have. For instance, you could do freelance work in writing music for productions or advertisements if you are a musician or do some freelance English teaching if you are an academic. Further, if you have other skills like writing or manual labor, you can pick up jobs online and make perfect money through numerous projects.

The benefit of freelance work is that you don't necessarily have to stick to one skill set. Using the numerous freelance work platforms available nowadays, such as Fiverr.com, Upwork.com, Freelancer.com, Peopleperhour.com, Writeraccess.com, and Freelancewriting.com, you can find side gigs that are suitable for your range of skills. When it comes to freelancing, you can pick up as many or as little gigs as you'd like and schedule them around your music. These websites above offer freelancers multiple different ways to make money. You could act as a ghostwriter and help people write books on topics you know about, or you could help a YouTube artist create background music without copyright for their channel, or you could simply help someone run a specific errand and get paid for it. The world is yours, and you can choose whatever suits your skills best. Below are a few examples of what freelance work encompasses.

Online Freelance Platforms

Fiverr.com
Fiverr.com is a platform that connects freelancers with specific skills to clients that require them. Most of the freelance skills on this website are more tech-related, including logo design, WordPress, social media, SEO, and illustrations. If you have experience in design and in technology (e.g., programming), then a lot of this work will be relevant to your skillset. They also offer different categories of skills, such as translation, data entry, book covers, and voice-overs. This could be a great way for you to build a freelance business.

Upwork.com
Upwork.com is a platform that is similar to Fiverr that connects freelancers with specific skills to clients or agencies that require them. The categories that are included in Upwork are broader than Fiverr and include; Web, Mobile and Software development, Design & Creative, Writing, Sales & Marketing, Admin Support, Customer Service, Data Science and Analytics, and Engineering and Architecture. Some of these categories may require you to have the education and professional experience, but the categories such as Writing and Customer service may not. Any individual or agency can post freelance work gigs on Upwork.com to find the right person to fulfill their needs. This opens it up to big companies that may be looking to hire someone for multiple projects that require the same skillset. Most of these gigs are all done remotely, so you can still maintain a flexible schedule and working

environment, which will allow you to keep working on your music.

Freelancer.com

Freelancer.com is similar to Upwork and Fiverr in the sense that it connects freelancers with specific skills to certain projects that require them. The most popular projects that freelancer.com receives include; website development, graphic design, Logo design, marketing, writing, and mobile app development. However, they have a huge selection of less popular categories but still have numerous projects posted daily. If you have any marketing experience or create logos, you may find projects that require those skills and apply to pick them up with this experience.

They also offer writing projects on this platform, so if you have experience writing articles, blogs, or e-books, this is the place to go to see what types of projects are available. Projects can range from $100 to over $500 + depending on the project size and skill type.

Peopleperhour.com

Peopleperhour.com is similar to the above platforms as it connects freelancers to projects and businesses that are looking for a certain skill. The most popular projects on this platform include video shooting experts, Go developers, Children book illustrators, appointment setters, Swift developers, Visual merchandisers, Arabic translators, interior designers, music composers, and wealth managers. As you can see, music composer is a part of their most popular categories – this may be right up your alley.

Tons of businesses and individuals are looking for people who can compose songs that they can use for their advertising or videos without copyright, so it doesn't get taken down on popular platforms like YouTube. Moreover, if you have experience shooting videos at concerts or if you know any other languages, you could look into those projects as they are popular on this platform. Specific to music composing, freelancers on this website are charging anywhere from $30 - $100+ per hour to compose original music.

Writeraccess.com
Writeraccess.com is different from the platforms that we just talked about as it is specific to writing, and you need to apply and get approved before you are matched with opportunities. If you are a strong writer and have experience writing blogs, books, articles, or e-books, then this is right up your alley. The genres of books offered on this site are endless as they have writers who can write about anything from agriculture to politics. For example, if you have special knowledge in a certain industry, you can use it to your writing advantage.

Freelancewriting.com
Freelancewriting.com is a platform that matches freelance writers to specific companies and individuals that require their services. The freelance work that is offered on this platform include; copywriting, content writing, project management, digital media management, SEO, RFP writing, and marketing. Writers can apply to these projects for free, while companies and individuals who seek these skills pay a fee to utilize their platform to find the right talent. All

of these jobs are done from the comfort of your home so that you can maintain your flexibility in terms of hours and location.

Editing and Proofreading

Suppose you are someone that has good writing and editing skills. In that case, proofreading and editing written documents is a great way for you to make some extra income. This is ideal for someone who may be in the field of writing and is looking to increase their own writing skills while making money at the same time. There isn't a single platform that is dedicated to this type of work, but with a quick google search, you can find a variety of freelance proofreading and editing gigs. You can usually make around $200 - $300 per written document depending on its length, so just proofreading a few documents per month can significantly increase your monthly income.

Temporary Side Gigs

In this section, we will be focusing solely on a type of side gig that is temporary and on an hourly basis. However, temporary side gigs are easily confused with the remote jobs side gig as those are also paid on an hourly wage basis.

The main difference here is that temporary side gigs require you to be on the job site in person, while remote gigs are done entirely from your own home. Although this type of work is not as flexible as remote gigs, it opens up to many more skillsets than remote work. Remote work is mainly limited to people within the technology field and business administration field, while hourly/temporary gigs could be anything from bartending to customer service. For instance, if you have experience working in restaurants and bars, you can advertise those skills on platforms catered to this type of work. Employers who require temporary service staff could reach out to you and hire you for a temporary gig. The main platforms used to connect freelancers to companies and individuals that require services include shiftgig.com, appleone.com, and Wonolo.com.

In terms of earning potential for temporary side gigs, you can expect at least the minimum wage requirement based on where you live. Depending on what types of jobs you get hired for, you have the potential to earn tips as well. People in positions like servers, bartenders, and baristas have the potential to make a lot of extra money just on tips alone. This is a reliable type of income as you will be guaranteed money for the number of hours you put in. Let's take a look at a few platforms that support this type of work.

Shiftgig.com is one of the most popular platforms for employers to seek out temporary/hourly employees for their business needs. The most commonly sought-after jobs on this website include; bartenders, servers, cooks, housekeepers, porters, call-center representatives, customer service representatives, warehouse packers, retail specialists, promo models, and brand ambassadors. In terms of flexibility, this type of side gig is not as flexible as remote jobs and project-based work. Employers will set the time you need to clock in and clock out just like any regular job, and you must abide by those hours. However, you are guaranteed an income for the number of hours you put in, unlike setting up your online store or course creation, where your income highly depends on how many people purchase your services and goods.

Moreover, once you do an excellent job for a specific employer in this field, there is a high likelihood that they will contact you again for their next business requirement. Many restaurants and coffee shops that do pop up stores during conferences shows and fairs need a temporary set of staff during their busy times of the year. Again, the earning potential is average here as the minimum amount you will be paid the minimum wage in your area, but specific jobs that require skills higher than entry-level can be paid from $20 or more.

The next platform you can look into is appleone.com, where it acts as a recruitment platform for employers to seek talent for the temporary work that they need. This platform supports virtually any type of job out there and is not specialized in anything in particular. Some recruiters work for this platform that reaches out to the applicant base to contact people who meet the employer's requirements. Just like shiftgig.com, the flexibility is not as great as other side gigs as you need to be at your workplace at the requested clock in time and clock out at your set time as well. However, the income will be steady as you would be working any regular job but just on a temporary and hourly status.

The number of hours you put in will equal the amount that you get paid.

The next platform we will be taking a look at is Wonolo.com. This platform is similar to shiftgig.com but is a little more specialized in terms of what types of employers and employees it's looking for. They typically specialize in warehouse operations, general labor, delivery drivers, food production, event staffing, washing, cleaning, administrative, and merchandising. They pre-screen candidates and allow them to create a profile on the platform, and they get matched with opportunities that employers post. The earning potential is relatively high with Wonolo as the pay rates range from $15 per hour to $20 per hour, depending on what your skillset is. It has the same flexibility level as the two other platforms we just learned about. Still, Wonolo is one of the biggest platforms in temporary/hourly staffing, so that you may find the most opportunities there.

If you have a range of skills or are simply just okay with doing some manual labor work, you can easily find gigs on Wonolo to help you pay your bills.

Overall, temporary/hourly side gig work is not much different than having a part-time job. The only difference is that you have more flexibility regarding when you can pick up work, but you still have to follow the employer's schedule based on their needs. If you have a reasonably flexible schedule and can physically be on a job site for a few days a week, this is one of the safest and most reliable sources of income out there.

Remember, you can take on multiple side gigs at once to create different sources of revenue. You can be running an online store while picking up some warehouse working shifts to generate cash flow. Don't be tunnel-visioned, and make sure that you have more than one stream of income at all times.

Chores

This type of side gig is one of the newer ones that emerged over the last couple of years. Platforms like TaskRabbit allow people to list a range of tasks/chores/errands they require help with and are willing to pay other people to do it for them. This can range from running simple errands like picking up some things from the grocery store to assembling their IKEA furniture to helping someone make home improvements. This can make you a good amount of money if you have some useful life skills that you could charge money for. For instance, I hate building furniture, so I would happily pay a handy person a fair price to build my furniture for me. The average reported monthly income for TaskRabbit is around $110, which isn't a lot but could be an interesting side hustle for you to complement with others.

Cleaning

Similar to the above side gig, cleaning is another good option. Cleaning as a side gig is something anyone can do as long as you are someone who gains the satisfaction of turning a messy/dirty place into a clean and sparkling one. There is nearly no start-up cost, as most clients who hire this type of service provide the cleaning equipment and supplies. However, in the scenario that you are required to bring your own tools, they are cheap, and you likely have them in your own home already. Depending on where you live, there can be many people seeking cleaning services or not many at all. In big metropolitan cities where it's condominium and apartment galore, there are tons of clients that are seeking reliable and trustworthy cleaners to come in a few times a month to keep their place tidy. Moreover, if you live in a dense city, there are always renters and tenants moving in and out of homes, which opens up the market for landlords to hire cleaning staff to clean units before somebody new moves in.

You can find this type of work using websites such as Tidy.com, taskrabbit.com, and craigslist.com. You can even simplify this further and create your own ad on your local buy/sell groups offering your cleaning services at an hourly rate. You can offer different types of services related to cleaning at different prices. For instance, a routine weekly/monthly cleaning can be charged less than a yearly deep clean. You can also reach out to Airbnb owners and offer them your services as they need a cleaning person to come and remake units when the clients check out. Tidy.com helps clients get matched with home keepers and cleaners in their area; this includes Airbnb owners as well. Depending on what type of client you find or the agency that connects you, most cleaners make around $25/hour (2 − 3 hours per clean) or $100+ per unit cleaned. Those rates are specific to cleaning apartments and condominiums, but house cleaning wages start at $25/hour (4+ hours per clean) or $200 per unit.

Although Tidy.com, taskrabbit.com, and craigslist.com are good places to start looking for cleaning side gigs, you can research your own cleaning companies based out of your local neighborhood. Suppose you want to maximize your earning potential and not have to give a cut to any agency or company. In that case, you can build your own service and post flyers in local condominiums and apartments the old fashioned way to generate business. This type of work is ideal for those who enjoy cleaning and don't have the time to work for more than a few hours at a time. The scheduling is also quite flexible, so you can choose to schedule cleaning for your clients when you are not practicing music.

Moreover, this type of side gig is fairly reliable as once you do good work for a few clients, they'll likely routinely hire you every single week and month to upkeep their home. If you clean three units a week at $25/h, and it takes you about 2 hours per session, then you are making $150 per week and $600 per month. This is good money considering you only worked 6 hours per week!

If you believe cleaning and home-keeping are right up your alley, my recommendation would be to start off cleaning through an agency or platform like tidy.com to gain some experience and refine your skills. They pay reasonable rates, but you could make more if you went completely independent. Once your skills have been refined and you are 100% sure that this is the perfect side gig for you, I advise you to open up your own cleaning business and open up your client base to cleaning for move-in/move-outs for condos and houses, Airbnb checks in/check out cleaning, deep cleaning services, and weekly/monthly routine upkeeping. By establishing your own business, you build credibility with your repeat customers and guarantee yourself a steady income with a set client base.

Organizing
Organizing is a great side gig for those who find joy in keeping tidy and neat. Organizing side gigs can range from helping people sort out the junk from their home to organizing someone's pantry to installing fixtures or furniture in someone's home. If you are reasonably handy and comfortable with tasks that require manual labor, you may find yourself enjoying side gigs within the home organization field. Don't get mixed up; however, these jobs aren't solely just organizing people's homes; it goes as far as helping others remove tree limbs from their lawn or pressuring washing someone's desk or backyard. Most of these side gigs do require you to have your equipment but very minimally. For instance, you can do all organization tasks with just your hands, so there is no start-up cost there, but if you are helping someone set up a new table or bookshelf, you may need to bring your toolbox.

Platforms that help connect clients with people who do this type of work include Takl.com and Thumbtack.com. Takl.com focuses more on side gigs related to someone's home or property, while thumbtack.com opens it up to people who may need help with other locations that aren't just limited to their homes. For instance, Takl.com already has a list of providers (people who are doing this for side gigs) that are ready to get paid for doing tasks like; mowing the client's lawn, cleaning their homes, hanging a light fixture, hauling away old appliances, mounting a TV, reorganizing furniture at home, cleaning out gutters, installing curtain rods and cleaning outside areas of a person's home.

If you register yourself as a provider and list all the skills you have, this platform can help you match yourself with clients requiring your assistance. This is especially good for someone who has a broad range of skills but not necessarily one primary talent with a large client base. For instance, you may be someone who is handy but is also good at cleaning. Instead of limiting yourself to platforms that are solely specialized in either space, Takl.com can help match you with every job related to every skill you have. Moreover, the scheduling is quite flexible with Takl, so you can schedule projects and clients whenever you are available. If your other job requires you to be flexible in terms of your schedule, you will find this helpful as you can plan your clients around your availability. Moreover, depending on your past job experience, you may have experience hauling equipment to and from locations, so moving around some furniture to help clients reorganize their living room should be an easy task and a quick way to make some cash.

It's hard to precisely identify the earning potential with Takl because it depends on what skill sets you are bringing to the table and what the clients are willing to pay. However, you can likely expect $20 per hour for most tasks, but they can also pay per project.

Thumbtack is a similar platform to Takl, but it opens it up to more services that are catered to different businesses and people rather than specializing in residential homes. Thumbtack helps clients connect to people like you that have experience in home remodeling (tiling, flooring, general contracting work), home maintenance (cleaning, painting, handymen), weddings (photographers, wedding officiants, makeup artists), events (caterers, DJs), interior design, lawn work, and roof repair and maintenance. If you are creative, you may be able to try your luck at DJ gigs that pay a reasonable amount if you have experience with that type of work. Thumbtack is a suitable medium for taking your side gig work and building it into your own side business. If you have the right certifications, skills, and equipment, you can undercut many professional companies when it comes to contracting work and weddings.

Some people have reported starting earnings to be between $500 - $1000, picking up projects paying over $3000 per month in terms of earning potential. Again, it highly depends on what your skills are and what equipment you have available. Still, if you develop a desirable skill within contracting and maintenance, you can make some serious cash.

Takl.com and Thumbtack.com are platforms that offer fantastic resources to people who are interested in a side gig. The highest-paying jobs are the ones that require handy skills like tiling, painting, and maintenance. If you know your way around different cables and connectivity, this would be an excellent choice for you. If this is the side gig route you want to go, start practicing your handy skills by picking up smaller home-projects on Takl.com, and you can move on and pick up more extensive projects and open up your client and project base on thumbtack.com. Remember, skills that require training like tiling and maintenance work are expensive for people to purchase at a commercial level. By learning these types of skills and refining them, you will find a lot of business in these areas if you slightly undercut those businesses.

Depending on what projects you pick up from these websites, they can range from being reasonably flexible to highly inflexible. For instance, if you pick up a kitchen tiling job, you likely have to work 1 – 2 full days to get it done as the client would not want the tiling to go on for more than a few days due to inconvenience. Needing these two days means that you would need 1 – 2 entire days off from your regular work to complete these projects. However, if you were picking up projects like pressure washing a deck or installing a light fixture, these jobs will be done in a few hours, and the client can be more flexible regarding when you can come and go.

Chapter 8: Property Rentals

This chapter will expand on our chapter five discussion of trading and investment options. This chapter will look at property rentals and real estate investments and how you can make quick, passive income from these.

Managing a property rental is a great option for a side gig. This method is perfect for someone who has an extra property or an extra room in their house/apartment. Various property rentals can earn you passive income, including long and short-term rental agreements. We will look at examples of each below.

Long-Term Rentals

The first type of income that you can earn from renting property is by being a Landlord. To do this, you can list a room, a house, or an apartment on any rental site, like craigslist, and find a tenant to rent your place by making monthly payments for a yearly contract.

Being a landlord allows you to make passive income by simply collecting rent payments every month. This method is a great, hassle-free, and hands-off way to make passive income. This is arguably the best way to make additional income because it allows you to pursue other endeavors like owning a business or working a day job while making rental income without putting in much effort. The only time that you would be required to earn your income actively is when your tenants need something or when you need to find tenants to rent actively. Once you sign a 12-month contract with your tenants, however, you do not have to do much else.

Short-Term Rentals

Vacation rentals
Vacation rentals are a growing form of side-hustle, especially for people who live in high-rent cities like New York City, San Francisco, or Toronto. You can make vacation rentals a larger source of your income if you have a spare room in your home or a property that you can fix up to be rented.

Renting out your room/unit on a nightly basis can make you anywhere from $50 - $250 per night. Some people decide to rent a room in their apartment from Friday – Sunday, as most people use the weekend to have a getaway. This method allows you to maintain your vacation rental property away from your day job while making anywhere from $150/weekend to $600/weekend. You also have the flexibility of setting your nightly price, so dates with higher demand like Christmas or Spring break can be listed at a higher nightly price.

Airbnb
Instead of paying rent or mortgage to your home while you are away, you can list it as an Airbnb or HomeAway

rental for tourists or travelers to rent. Due to the increasing cost of nearly everything, people nowadays prefer to book an Airbnb compared to a hotel to save money by having the amenities to cook their food and fit more people into one space.

Event Space Rentals
Another side gig that is a great source of passive income is to rent out event space. This way, you collect a fee for people who want to use your space to host events such as parties, weddings, or anything else. This passive income source can make you a lot of money with very minimal work required on your part.

Commercial Property Rentals
If you can afford to buy a commercial property, you can rent it out to someone who wants to use the space to run a business. This kind of property requires more money upfront than a traditional house purchase, but it can provide you with great rewards in the long-run if you can hold onto it and collect rental income. This kind of property has the potential to provide you with the job of a full-time landlord if you can make enough income from it.

Rental Property Income Potential

If you are renting out a room or a unit in a house, you could easily charge upwards of $50 per night. This depends on where you live, as you must match your rate to the market value in the city or general location where your house is located. In some places, people charge up to $250 per night. With this range, your income potential could amount to a weekly income of $150 - $750 if you rent a space in your own home from Friday – Monday. Of course, if you rent an entire house or cottage, you can get more money per night, depending on how many rooms the house has. People can charge up to and beyond $600 USD per night in the most desirable locations for people to vacation. If you can manage to fill your month by having back-to-back rentals, this could bring you upwards of $18000 before Airbnb fees come out (if that is the platform you choose). As you can see, the income potential comes with a vast range of values, so it is difficult to say exactly how much you could make.

Buying and Selling Property

As I mentioned, renting a property is one great way to turn an investment property into a passive income source. In addition to providing you with income, it could also cover your mortgage payments for you while you wait for your house's value to grow. When this happens, you can sell, and you will make a lump-sum of money that you earned passively.

Tips for Investing in Income Properties

As I mentioned, investing in a property is a great and secure way to grow your money in the long-term. If you are in a position to buy a property, I strongly suggest it. Even if you are not ready to live in a property that you own, there are numerous ways to turn this into a passive income source for yourself. One way to turn this into passive income is by using it as a rental property. Doing this can bring you rental income or cover your mortgage payments for you. The second way is by simply investing your money and waiting for your house's value to grow. When this happens, you can sell, and you will make a lump-sum of money that you earned passively.

It can be challenging to make enough money to invest in a property, but any of the side gigs in this book can help you to earn and save passive income that will bring you closer to buying a property. For example, if you had enough money for a down payment for a property, think $50,000 - $100,000 at least, then you could invest in a home and turn it into a property where it generates rental income for you. Let's say you got a decent mortgage from your local bank, and you put down a $50,000 down payment for a $300,000 home. Now let's say you agreed to a monthly payment of $2,500 to your bank plus a 2.5% interest rate for ten years, which leads you to pay around $2560 a month. Since property prices tend to increase with time depending on where you live naturally, it's safe to say that your $300,000 investment could become a $400,000 investment in a few years. If you rent out your new property to tenants that cover the full mortgage ($2560), this means that you are no longer making payments to the bank, the tenants are, and you get to keep your money growing on your property. By spending $50,000 on your down payment, you are generating over $300,000 of income over the next few years with a high likelihood of it becoming a property that is worth way more than $300k in a few years. Let's say in 5 years your property value has increased to $450,000. By doing nothing at all, you have paid off $125,000 ($2500 per month x 5 years), and the value of your house has grown by $150,000. Therefore, in just five years, with minimal work, you have made $275,000. For some people, that is a decent salary of $55,000 a year for five years. All of this was made by simply having enough resources to build a strong passive income stream.

How to Choose a Property Type

In this section, I will break down the different types of real estate investment properties so that you can decide which is the best option for you.

Rental Properties
As discussed previously, this is one of the most popular forms of real estate investment. This kind of real estate investment is when a person buys a property intending to hold onto it and rent it out for rental income. This property could include a condo, a house, an apartment complex, or a building used as an event space.

House Flipping
House flipping is another option for investing and making quick money through real estate, but this method requires skill and expertise.

To do this, some people invest in real estate by purchasing a house for little money, fixing it up for as little cost as possible, and quickly selling it at a much higher price than purchasing it. This kind of real estate investment provides people with quick lump sums of profit, but it requires them to be build-savvy and work quickly, under pressure.

Real Estate Investment Groups
This kind of real estate investment involves a small mutual fund that purchases rental properties. People can then purchase units or apartments from the company that purchased the entire property. Once a person has purchased a unit or several units, the company in charge of the property will rent them to tenants. In this case, the real estate company will take care of all logistics involved in renting a property, from advertising to maintenance and everything in between.

Which Kind of Property Can Make the Most Income?

Below you can see which real estate investment properties are the most lucrative, which will help you choose which type of property you should invest your money into.

Commercial Real Estate
Commercial real estate includes a variety of different commercially available spaces such as:

- Office space
- Industrial space
- Parking spaces and parking lots

- Retail space
- Restaurant and service industry space
- Etc.

Commercial real estate involves renting to businesses, which is generally a smoother process than renting to individuals for residential purposes. Further, as a commercial landlord, you can charge much higher prices, especially if your space is in a highly desirable location.

Residential Rental Real Estate
Residential real estate is the second most desirable type of rental property. This kind of investment involves renting your property monthly to an individual every month, collecting rent, and acting as the landlord. This kind of rental can offer high income, as the tenants can pay your mortgage while your property value increases.

Properties For Flipping
The third most lucrative kind of real estate investment is the "fixer-upper" or the house flipping type of investment. This kind of investment can provide you with quick income. Still, it relies on your ability to work quickly and efficiently and your ability to fix up and renovate the property according to code and potential buyer's preferences.

Benefits of Property Income

It can be challenging to make enough money to invest in a property, but any of the side gigs in this book can help you to earn and save passive income that will bring you closer to buying a property. However, compared to other forms of investments, real estate is said to be one of the most reliable and secure. This kind of investment is great for those who are risk-averse and have the money to invest in a tangible, reliable investment. For this reason, if you can afford to buy a property, you will see returns on your investment.

Notes for Success

Now that you understand a little more about what real estate investment entails and how it can benefit you in numerous ways, I will share some tips for success in this realm of investing.

Plan Ahead
When investing, it is important to plan ahead in every sense of the word. Plan ahead when it comes to your money, your responsibilities, your risks, and your finances.

Research the Market
Before investing, it is important to research the market to make informed and educated decisions regarding your properties, buying, and selling. Be sure to look at projections for the future.

Maintain ethical investing standards
While you may get by using illegal or unethical tactics in real estate investing, this will not bring you long-lasting success. Since you are looking for early retirement, you want a plan that you can follow for years to come, so stay ethical.

Find a niche for yourself.
As we discussed in this chapter, there are various real estate niches that you can focus on. Find one for yourself and work up to becoming a boss in that niche.

Always keep yourself up-to-date.
You must stay up to date when using investing as a main source of your income. Don't sleep on the current statistics, market trends, or any other world events. Keep yourself informed.

Know the risks you are taking
As with any type of investing, you must know and evaluate the risks at each step of the way. Ensure that you know what risks you are taking before you take them.

Hire a Team of Professionals
You don't have to be an expert in every part of the real estate investment process. You will thank yourself later. On that note, don't be afraid to hire an entire team of professionals to help you at every step of the process. It will cost you some money, but it will pay off in the long run if things are done the right way and in a timely manner.

Find a mentor
Find yourself a mentor whom you can trust; it will make this process much smoother for you.

Chapter 9: Online Teaching and Coaching

This chapter will explore quick money-making methods that involve education, teaching, and tutoring. In our modern society, there is more than one way to learn a certain topic. Popular subjects like language, especially English, are often taught by people in America, Canada, and Europe to people from other countries who want to learn English. Moreover, online tutoring and in-person tutoring are a popular income method, especially centering on topics like math, science, and language studies. As long as you have some post-secondary education, you will qualify for most online teaching and tutoring jobs, and they can prove to be a great way to make quick money!

Tutoring Platforms

Let's talk a little about tutoring first, as this is the least intensive side gig in this chapter. Tutoring is an amazing side gig that can bring you a significant amount of income. You can find these opportunities through independent tutoring companies or online platforms like Wyzant and GlassGap.

Tutoring can be done in-person or online, depending on your preferences. Online tutoring is more flexible as you can do it from your home. Online tutoring is essentially the same as in-person tutoring except for the fact that you are doing it over video chat rather than sitting face-to-face. With online tutoring, the possibility of subjects widens even more. Now you have different options like teaching multiple languages or other subjects that may differ from what your local tutoring schools are teaching. Some of the most well-known tutoring platforms include tutor.com and pearson.com.

Depending on your education level, you could tutor students in elementary, high-school, and post-secondary schools. The higher the education level you teach, the higher you will get paid on an hourly basis. You can look at some online tutoring opportunities by looking them up based on where you live or starting with the online platforms that I will discuss below. If there are many high schools or well-known universities in your area, the chances are that many businesses or families are looking to hire tutors for various subjects. Moreover, if you have specific skills in a given area, you can also look into businesses looking to hire online teachers or tutors in that area.

The above options are highly dependent on where you are located, so you can spend your own time researching which options exist in your city. Let's take a look at each platform and see what they have to offer.

Tutor.com
Tutor.com is a large platform that offers tutoring services in pretty much every subject imaginable. The subjects that they cover include:

- Math (everything from algebra to calculus to statistics to middle-grade math)
- Science (biology, chemistry, physics)
- English
- Social studies
- AP support (calculus, physics, biology)
- SAT prep, foreign languages, and business.

In terms of earning potential, online tutoring does not pay as much as in-person tutoring because you need to go through an agency rather than finding clients on your own. Many tutors report making around $15 per hour using tutor.com, which is significantly less than tutoring in person. However, the flexibility is much higher, so you wouldn't need to leave the comfort of your own home, and you can build your schedule much easier.

Pearson.com
Pearson.com is a unique way to make money in the tutoring/teaching field. Rather than teaching students on various subjects, Pearson hires many online test-scorers to mark tests and exams. Virtually anyone can do this.

The one downfall to this is that the earning potential is much lower compared to teaching and tutoring. Most Pearson test scorers make anywhere from $12 - $13 per hour. However, you do get the benefit of working from home, so you get to enjoy your flexibility.

Lastly, since tests only happen at certain times of the year, there will be times where there isn't much to do, so this is not a steady side gig that can generate your income all year round. Tutoring and teaching can give you a steady flow of money throughout most of the year, but test marking and grading will only happen for a few months of the year, between September – August.

Language Instruction

As you are now aware, tutoring subjects can range from school subjects like math and science to teaching languages. English teaching is a quickly growing side hustle that can make you enough money to live on full-time.

VIPKid

VIPKid is an online English teaching platform. VIPKid pays its online English teachers anywhere from $17 - $22 per hour. The beauty of teaching English online is that you don't even have to leave the comfort of your own home, and you can choose which hours work for you. Meanwhile, tutoring can be done online or in-person, depending on which company you work for. If you are tutoring for a high school student, the average tutor gets paid anywhere between $30 - $40 per hour. Just by doing 10 hours of it a week can bring you $300 - $400 per week of extra income; that's $900 - $1600 per month.

Online Course Creation and Instruction

This type of side gig is a new addition to the world of side gigs and has increased in popularity over the last 1 – 2 years. These types of platforms offer courses to people who require them to qualify for jobs and further education. Platforms like udemy.com, teachable.com, and foundr.com offer courses that are made by other people at a discounted rate to either help people catch up on their credits or give them a certification that will allow them to qualify for their line of work.

Skillshare
Skillshare is an example of a platform that allows you to make passive income by simply creating courses for others to learn things you are passionate about. This platform is a great way to make money on the side, as you simply create a course, upload it and wait for people to purchase it. This way, you can sit back and make money once you create your course, and once it is completed and uploaded, you are finished. You can make as many or as few courses as you like, depending on how many areas of expertise you have. Skillshare is primarily focused on creative industries. For example, there are photography courses, graphic design, drawing, photoshop, animation, productivity, etc.

Thinkific
Thinkific is similar to Skillshare in that you create and upload courses, but Thinkific contains a much wider variety of course material. For example, sports and fitness, cooking, music instruction, business, marketing, and even things as specific as food

photography. There is something for everyone on Thinkific, which is why this is a great option for people with niche skills or knowledge areas, especially if you have several different areas of knowledge that you can work with.

Udemy.com
Specific to Udemy.com, you can build your courses on virtually any topic possible and charge a price that you deem fair. You will get paid depending on how many people pay for your courses. Some courses are worth more than others, and people report to make anywhere between $1500 - $3000 per month for their work. This income is highly dependent on how much you promote your courses and how many people require this type of training. In some ways, if you are only selling your course work, I would say Udemy.com is a great way to generate passive income because you won't have to do much after posting your course online for sale. However, it is not a reliable source of income as your pay will change drastically depending on how many purchases you get that month. I would keep this type of work as a source of passive income and have multiple other active income sources to generate the cash flow you need. This method definitely won't hurt to try out, especially if you already have course material at hand that you know inside and out. For instance, if you are a musician, you may know the basics of music and scales inside and out, so it will take you not much time to create a solid music foundation course.

Teachable.com
Let's talk a little about teachable.com. Teachable.com is a platform where a person can sell and create online courses for free. It allows you to build your own course website, host your content, and charge students interested in it for the course when they purchase it. Again, this is similar to Udemy as it's a great source of passive income because once you finish building your course, all you have to do is wait for it to be purchased. However, the business will heavily depend on your course's popularity and how many prospective students are in the realm of what your course offers. It is unknown so far for teachable in terms of earning potential due to the high variance from person to person. You can essentially make $0 if your course does not generate any students or interest, but some people have made over $18,000 in less than a month due to their course popularity. I'd like to drill in the point that this is a great way as a passive source of income but is highly unreliable if you want to make it your active side hustle source.

Foundr.com
Foundr.com is a resource aimed at people looking to build their own online business but need the guidance and knowledge others possess. Using the Foundr platform, you can make money by posting courses, articles, and teaching blogs about how one can jumpstart their own business. This platform isn't as popular compared to udemy and teachable due to its specialized nature. In Udemy and teachable, you can create and sell courses for virtually everything, while

Foundr is focused on content related to entrepreneurship.

If you are a creative person, you may or may not have experience in this area. My recommendation would be to utilize the skills you already have through your previous education or your music skills, create courses that you're familiar with at ease, and put them up for sale as a type of passive income.

Create Your Own Course or Lesson Teaching Business
Another option you have that is similar to the above is to create courses that you can benefit from as a passive income source, but doing so without using a platform. That way, you won't have to pay fees to the platform to host your courses.

The challenge here will be finding clients to purchase your courses, but if you are confident that you can develop leads and find business, this could be a great option for you. You can do this by hosting courses on your own website and including a payment option.

Lessons

Now that we have covered all the in-person teaching options, let's look into some online music teaching platforms. The largest and most popular platform for this type of work is lessons.com. Lessons.com is specialized in music teaching and offers teaching in sports, dance, health, fitness, martial arts, cooking, driving, painting, and many more. As a teacher, you can post your subject of expertise and have students pay to sign up for your classes.

Lessons.com's earning potential varies a lot as it depends on how many people sign on to them. As a teacher, this platform allows you to contact potential students looking for specific lessons and send a quote for your services. This is mostly done online and is extremely flexible.

Online Coaching

This section will focus on another specific type of teaching or tutoring side hustle – coaching. To begin, I will explain what coaching entails. One way to become a coach is to start your own coaching business, where you act as both the coach and the administrator. In this business, you will need to find clients that you feel you can help.

Ideally, you must have a plethora of experience in the field of coaching that you are looking to specialize in. If you have been in the workforce for a while or have a good education, there is likely a niche of coaching that you would be suitable for. For instance, some people who found success working in a sales job may be interested in starting a business coaching side hustle. In comparison, someone who has found success as a Yoga teacher or enthusiast may be interested in starting a spiritual coaching business.

We will get more specific later in this section when we learn about different types of coaching opportunities. There are many different types of coaching businesses, and there is something for everyone; it is just a matter of finding out what makes the most sense for your knowledge and skills.

Most people hire a coach to help them with specific projects, transitions, or personal goals. The coach's responsibility is to help you grow by assessing your current situation, limiting beliefs, and other challenges. The coach will then create a customized plan that they design to help you achieve your goals.
If you are thinking about starting your own coaching business in the first place, you probably want to know how coaching compares to a career during these unstable times of the economy. The best part about this is that coaching is gaining an excellent reputation as a profession, probably because of the uncertainties in our economy, forced career changes, and businesses' drastic efforts to make their operations more efficient and productive during numerous financial challenges. In terms of statistics, the coaching industry in 2012 brought i2 billion spread amongst approximately 50,000 coaches.

You may already know that coaches set their rates and their rates tend to differ a lot. Some coaches may charge $25 per hour, while some may charge $300+ per hour. After coming out from a certification program, the standard hourly rates for certain coaches can be anywhere from $100 per hour to $150 per hour.

The most significant differentiating factor between coaching rates depends on the type of coaching that you are doing. Although there are numerous different coaching types, the industry includes life coaching, business coaching, and executive coaching.

A recent study on the coaching industry found that the average income for coaches who worked full time was over $80,000. For coaches who did it part-time, it brought in revenue of around $25,000 per year. For you to have a good understanding of what type of coaching brings in the most income, let's take a look at some of the top coaches in our industry today that are making over $100,000.

This section will learn about the different opportunities that exist if you are thinking of choosing coaching as your side hustle. There are many different types of coaching side hustles to choose from, and this section will help you narrow down your choices based on your experience and expertise.

Corporate/ Career Coaching

Career coaches are focused on helping people that are seeking career advice. These coaches use a very solution-oriented approach to help these people define, redefine, and achieve their goals related to their current working situation's professional objectives. For example, a career coach can help people figure out what type of job they're looking for next to grow their careers. They specialize in giving people advice based on what their current working situation is. They could be executives, employees, or freelancers. Regardless, career coaches help these people develop skills like leadership, stress management, self-confidence, interpersonal skills, and conflict-management skills. Depending on the clients' needs, the career coach's responsibilities, tasks, and services will differ accordingly, but the core coaching process is still the same in all cases.

Financial Coaching

A financial coach is responsible for helping their clients with money management basics. They work with clients struggling with their money management or those who simply have an unhealthy relationship with money. A financial coach's primary responsibility is to help their clients develop better and healthier money managing habits that are sustainable. Financial coaches spend a lot of time educating their clients on personal finance basics and work hand-in-hand with them to create a financial plan to help them achieve their personal goals. They also focus heavily on empowering their clients to be responsible for their spending actions and help them develop accountability for themselves.

Typically, financial coaches work with each client for several weeks. They would meet with their clients every week to advise them on their finances and check in on their progress.

The process that financial coaches use typically consists of three steps. The first step is to help them become more aware of their spending habits by tracking their spending to see for themselves. The second step is to help the client build their own financial goals, whether it's to pay off debt, save up for a property, or simply create a budget. The last step in this process is for the financial coach to help their clients build out sustainable plans and hold them accountable to follow those plans.

You might be wondering what the difference is between a financial coach and a financial advisor at this point. The main difference is that a financial coach helps teach those who aren't strong in money and finance management to better manage their money. In contrast, financial advisors advise you on growing and investing your money. Typically, financial coaches work with clients who don't have many assets and need to generate more financial stability for themselves. In contrast, financial advisors usually make their money by charging a percentage of the money your assets are generating. Financial coaches usually charge by the hour or have a flat retainer fee.

Financial coaching has the flexibility of being done in person, over the phone, or via video conferencing. The kind of meetings you hold is quite flexible as there isn't a need for the financial coach to see the client face to face. Since these sessions' purpose is to focus on money management, there isn't a need to be face-to-face.

If you think financial coaching is your niche, you may be interested in specializing in it even further. You could specialize your financial coaching services towards people looking to get out of debt or looking to save up for a down payment, or those who simply are bad with money. You can identify which further specializations are the most suitable for you by assessing your own experience. Have you ever experienced getting yourself out of debt? Have you ever saved up for your down payment? Or are you someone who used to be terrible with their money but now have multiple assets? These are all things you could consider before choosing what your coaching type will be.

Performance Coaching
Performance coaches are focused on helping clients who need to improve their performance or abilities for a specific task they have or want a career in, like sports. However, performance coaching helps both athletes and non-athletes alike.

For instance, writers can use performance coaches to get an idea of their full potential when it comes to writing. The performance coach can help assess where they are in terms of their writing skill, assess their work, and help guide the client toward creating a vision and a set of goals that can be accompanied by an action plan.

Performance coaching is one of those coaching types where it's almost necessary to specialize even further. Some performance coaches only coach people in the performing arts like ballet, while other performance coaches may focus on half-pipe snowboarding.

Performance coaches are responsible for facilitating conversations with their clients so that the clients are encouraged to set goals that are achievable and are working towards a larger goal. These coaches also help their clients build their self-awareness to identify and overcome any challenges and obstacles they may face when looking to improve their desired skills.

If you are looking to do performance coaching, it is ideal for specializing even further within a skill that you are confident you have a lot of knowledge. For instance, if you have been a snowboarder your whole life and want your side hustle to be performance coaching, it will be beneficial for you to advertise your coaching business as performance coaching specializing in snowboarding. Due to your history and experience with this sport, you can gain a lot of credibility when marketing your services and pitching your ideas to clients.

Performance coaching can be done individually, in groups, or in corporate situations. Most of the time, it is done individually, but corporate companies may seek out this type of service. For instance, dance studios or boot camp companies may seek out a performance coach to help their clients further build upon their skills.

Spiritual Coaching
A spiritual coach focuses on helping the client connect with their inner-self. These coaches help their clients change, navigate, and re-direct their lives to discover their desires, goals, dreams, and break out of any limiting beliefs. Unlike the other types of coaching we've discussed, spiritual coaching's main goal is to help people get in touch with themselves. A person may want to get in touch with themselves because they have lost their way in life and need to re-discover who they are. It could be someone who's gone through an impactful experience and want to explore new beginnings.

Spiritual coaches use a more holistic approach with their clients. They tend to help their clients discover their operating system that is under their consciousness. Spiritual coaches help people discover more than just who they are on the surface.

Spiritual coaching helps the client discover their depth and helps guide the client as they journey through self-discovery. All these changes run deeper than just surface level, but they all involve finding the underlying understanding of a person's being that contributes to long-lasting happiness.

Spiritual coaching can happen in person, over the phone, and via video conferencing. It can also be in the form of individual sessions, group sessions, and corporate sessions. Since spiritual coaches focus on everything below the surface, there isn't a need for sessions to happen in person, so normally sessions over the phone will suffice. If you think that spiritual coaching is your niche, you know what I'm about to say next – you can specialize even further. You can specialize in your spiritual coaching services to help people move on from trauma or help people break away from the norm and discover who their inner-self is. Remember, the best way to identify your second specialization is to look back onto your own experience and assess what areas you feel confident in coaching others.

Wellness or Nutrition and Fitness Coaching
Wellness coaches help their clients by assisting them in building sustainable and healthy behavior in their day to day lives. They do this by helping the clients identify their skills, strengths, and resources and help them create a vision of who they want to be and guide them towards it. This can include fitness coaching, nutrition coaching, or a holistic approach to wellness, depending on where your expertise lies and what your clients are looking for.

Like I mentioned numerous times, there isn't a prerequisite to becoming a coach. There is no prerequisite for becoming a wellness coach; anyone can do it as long as they are in a position where they can influence and help others through science-based tools. Wellness coaches help clients make changes to their present wellness. The clients can range from people who have a smoking or drinking habit to someone who is perfectly physically healthy but wants to improve their mental wellness.

Overall, course creation and instruction side gigs are beneficial to those who have a passion for teaching and are semi-skilled in course creation. This type of work gives the freelancer a great opportunity to make large sums of money, but there is a high-risk factor. If you put in 5 hours building your course for sale and you don't make any sales at all, then you just lost out on the time you put in when you could have used that time for other side gigs with a guaranteed return. As I mentioned throughout this chapter, it may not be the biggest income source if you use online course creations as your main income source. Instead, combining it with other sources and analyzing how well your sales are doing in the background before putting all your eggs in one basket may be better.

Keep in mind that flexibility is great in course creation gigs. Due to its nature, you can do this type of work anytime you want as long as you have a computer that will allow you to do so. There are no tight deadlines, and you can post courses for sale whenever you want. This option could be a very good option for a fairly busy creative who wants a passive income source to pay their bills.

Translation

If you are fluent in more than one language, you hold an extremely desirable skill to other people.

Platforms such as MotaWord and Unbabel help match multilingual people to clients that require their services. This is a side hustle that you can do from home or in person. Moreover, you can do these services, either translating words in real-time or translating written words like a book or an article. The income using these platforms ranges depending on the languages used and the type of work. However, many other companies or independent listings seek translation services if you are interested in this type of work.

Personal Trainer

This side hustle is also a very popular one and is so successful that many people have turned it into their main source of active income. If you are an ex-athlete or someone that is just well-versed in the world of fitness, you can make anywhere from $40 - $100 per hour training other people in the gym. This is even better if you are someone in the health and fitness field and can also use this side hustle experience to boost your own resume and career.

You can find clients in your own city by posting ads, or you can provide virtual training using platforms like GymGo. Keep in mind that most people like to work out in the mornings or after work, so your main working hours would likely be before 9 am or after 5 pm. If you train for 10 hours a week, you can make anywhere from $400 - $1000 per week, which is a monthly income of $1600 - $4000.

Chapter 10: How to Choose Which Income Source to Pursue

Side hustles are a great way to make extra money to pay off existing debt and to begin building a savings account that you can use to generate more money in the future. If you can accomplish these goals with passive income, while still working your day job, that is even better! This chapter will talk about how you can determine which secondary income source is best for you.

Considerations to Make Before Choosing

There are many different income sources to choose from; you can either build your own business or work on a freelance, contract, or on-call basis for another company. Some of these options are better suited to become passive income sources down the line, and some are better suited to become full-blown businesses down the line.

Keep in mind that a side hustle is different than a second job- as being employed as an "employee" simply means that you now have two jobs. However, picking up contracts or freelance work is a side-hustle because you get to choose how much you want to work and when you do it. Keep this in mind when choosing your secondary income source.

Take Stock of Your Resources

The first step in choosing a passive income source is to examine the resources you have access to. It is essential to talk about your current resources and examine whether you have enough resources to support the side job you are considering.

For instance, if you are interested in starting a business, you must be aware that it will not provide you with passive income right away, so you must make sure you have a secure day job that can support you while you get your side hustle going. Later in this chapter, we will discuss how you can transition from a day job to a full-time online income, but you must be aware that it will take time for now.

What are your Financial Resources?
If you have many resources to work with, it will be much easier for you to generate extra income. Have you ever heard the saying, "your first million is the hardest?" this is because money begins to make itself when you have enough of it.

If you are a person who has ample financial resources, you will likely be more interested in the financial realm of passive income, such as Stocks, Bonds, Commodities, and so on, or real estate income. If you have money to invest right now, you can essentially start making passive income immediately by investing it or beginning to trade stocks.

For instance, imagine you have a small fortune saved up, say $20,000. You can easily put that $20,000 into high-interest savings account at your local bank and generate 2-3% interest on it monthly. Doing this means that you are making $4,800 - $7,200 yearly by doing nothing at all. Although breaking it down into a monthly income, it's not much. That being said, simply just putting your money in a high-interest savings account can make you as much as any other new side hustle can. This method is the easiest way to make a passive income, but you could make even more money by doing other more elaborate things, such as buying a rental property or a car to rent out.

That being said, I understand that most people don't have $50,000 lying around to use as a down payment for a home, so I will spend most of this chapter talking about building a side hustle or a business that makes sense for you. Once this side hustle or business makes you enough money, then you can begin to invest it and grow it exponentially.

What are your Physical Resources?
The side gigs in this book will vary in terms of their individual start-up costs. Some may require you to invest in equipment or tools, while others only require your body! Depending on your resources, you may qualify for more or fewer of these options.

For example, are you able-bodied? Do you have some physical resources available already, like a video camera, a car, a second property, a computer, or equipment to run a business of your choice? These resources will influence your choices for starting a side hustle. Moreover, depending on your resources, it will open up doors for your side gig options. For instance, if you have a car, you will qualify to do numerous side gigs requiring a vehicle. If you have a spare house or property, this opens up multiple options for you as well. However, if you are someone with very limited resources, you may have to stick to the side gigs that don't require much equipment.

What Skills do you Have?
The next step to choosing a side hustle or a passive income source is to examine your skills.

If you have the skill to start a side business, this will provide you with a higher earning potential than a side hustle that does not require any specific skills. It is beneficial to consider that option first when choosing a side hustle, as it is more suitable for your knowledge, skills, and income.

For instance, many different side hustles out there, ranging from blog platforms to teaching personal training. These side hustles require specific skills and have the potential to earn you an extra income of $500 - $4000 per month.

Use Matching Platforms
Numerous platforms aim to match people with specific side hustles based on work skills in our modern world. Thanks to these platforms, about 10% of people have a side hustle in American households today.

Capitalize on your Interests and Experience
Any time someone is spending time doing something they enjoy, they are more likely to succeed. For this reason, think about what you enjoy and which of your life experiences may lend themselves to that job.

Throughout this book, I described numerous side gigs and their earning potential, and I also described what type of person this side gig is most suitable for. This information will help you decide on whether or not this side gig is ideal for you. Read back on the side gigs that spoke to you the most and evaluate yourself to determine whether you would be a good fit for that side gig.

In the scenario that you have started a side gig that you don't enjoy or doesn't meet the earning potential you imagined, then I encourage you to try a few others. Finding the perfect side gig that you enjoy pays well, and that allows you to balance your time takes trial and error. Don't give up just because the first side gig you tried didn't meet your expectations, try something else, and keep at it until you find one that works for you.

Tips for Success

I want to note that to find success in your side gigs, don't silo yourself into just one specific side gig. You should always have at least two side gigs ongoing. This way, if one gig is slow in business, you can focus on you're the other one. Having only one side gig puts you at the risk of not being able to pay your bills if it's slow in business for one month.

Further, keep in mind that the different side gigs featured in this book vary in popularity and earning potential depending on where you are located in the world. For instance, San Francisco will have many side gigs due to the high-tech and populated city compared to rural areas with a low population. If you are located in a big city, then luck is on your side. Most of these side gig suggestions will apply to you and will likely have a large client base. However, if you live in rural North Dakota, some of these side gigs will not make sense. Keep this in mind as you decide which side gig may be best for you.

People cannot achieve their financial goals without using self-discipline.

People cannot achieve their financial goals without self-discipline, so make sure you supplement your goals with a self-discipline list. It will help you focus on the tasks and behaviors you need to perform to achieve your goals. For example, one of your goals is to save $2,000 in 6 months. Your discipline list will include putting aside at least $350 every month and avoiding spending money on unnecessary things like fancy restaurants or video games. High self-discipline in this example would be doing everything on that list without any exception. It does not mean that you cannot reward yourself or take a break from working towards your goals; it simply means that you should get the things done on your list before indulging in any rewards.

Use a daily list to track your finances and to monitor unnecessary spending.
Make sure you are using a daily list to keep track of all the things you need to get done to achieve your goals. Try to use online tools or just a simple notebook that can help you prioritize and organize. It feels very satisfying to check off items that you've completed, and it will even motivate you to finish other tasks that are on your list just to feel the satisfaction of being able to check off another box. Make sure your to-do list works hand-in-hand with your discipline list to help yourself stay on track. A useful tip to keep in mind when you're feeling unmotivated is to start with the easiest item on the list just to get the ball rolling. Once you complete one easy task, people normally feel more motivated than before; this will help you get started on the rest of your list. Starting with a harder task may create apprehension about doing it; therefore, start small and work your way up.

Figure out which obstacles are holding you back from success.
Different people have different things that distract them from being able to complete important tasks. For example, a person that is easily distracted by emails and people in their office might have to close their office door as soon as they get into work to get their tasks done. They may delay any phone calls or meetings unless they're necessary for completing their set of responsibilities. This method is effective for people that may be trying to lose weight. For example, if they know that junk food is their weakness, instead of resisting eating junk food in their house, they can

simply eliminate all the junk food in their house, so they don't have access to it. You must minimize and remove all temptations of the distractions that affect you the most when reaching your most important goals.

Share your financial goals with other people.
It may be easier for some people to stick with completing a goal when they have made a public commitment. The thought of failing to reach a goal in front of other people can motivate them to stick with it. You can also take this one step further and ask those people to hold you accountable as well. If you aren't sharing your goals with anyone, nobody will know if you have been slacking off from it. When nobody is there to hold you accountable, you will likely be less motivated to keep doing it since nobody will know if you failed.

Use external sources or motivation as well as internal.
A saying goes, "don't do it for others; do it for yourself." However, some people find that they are much more disciplined when they know that their impulses, emotions, behaviors, and actions affect other people. Contrary to popular belief, it's alright to use external sources to help your motivation. Sometimes, motivation coming from external sources is more powerful than internal motivation. Find the purpose beyond yourself that is important to you to help give you a higher chance of success.

Discipline is created by creating habits.
When something becomes a habit, you no longer need to draw from your will power bank to get yourself to do it. For example, if your goal was to stop spending money at restaurants for lunch during the workday, get into the habit of making yourself fulfilling meals to prevent yourself from buying food when you're at the office. You will be able to see the benefits of saving money if you can stick with it. Once you see the benefit, you will have more motivation to keep doing it, and soon it becomes a habit where it will feel strange not to make your meals. This way, you will no longer need to draw from your bank of self-control, but instead, meal-prepping will come naturally since it has become a habit of yours.

Stop making excuses.
Don't procrastinate, or wait for tomorrow, do it now. If you fall off the wagon, that's okay. Start over immediately. Stop telling yourself that something is too hard, or there's something that you cannot change. Don't blame other people for the circumstances that you're in. Making excuses is the Kryptonite of self-discipline. Achieve a mindset that is more about "I can do this" rather than "I'll do it tomorrow."

How to Balance Online Income and Your Day Job

As I mentioned at the beginning of this new endeavor, you will need to work to build your side hustle in the hours that you are not working your day job. Due to this, your working hours for your side hustle will likely take place during weekends, evenings, or holidays. This will be taxing at first, but it will quickly become worth it when you begin to see the extra income flowing into your bank account.

If you have goals that require a lot of money, like buying a property or investing in stocks to trade, then creating multiple sources of passive income on top of your active income may be the ideal route. For this reason, you will likely need to spend a lot of time outside of your day job working to build this sum of money. The good news is that once you have it, you can relax and watch as your money makes more money in the form of ROI. ROI stands for "Return on Investment."

Whether you are an investor or business owner, return on investment is an important analytical tool that you will need to use. The definition of ROI is the relationship between a loss and a profit, which will be important to you when you begin to invest or as you build your own business.

ROI is described as an investment. This number is always written or described as a percentage increase or decrease related to the fiscal year's investment value. Here is a simple example: imagine that you invest $200 on stocks, and the value of those stocks increases to $220 by the end of that fiscal year. In this example, your ROI would be 10%. In one more complicated example, if you invested $1000 in coffee bean stock for your coffee business and at the end of the year you generated $2200 from selling coffee made by the beans (assuming no other costs or taxes are involved), your ROI is 220%.

What this means is that you will need to put in a lot of extra hours to build that initial sum of money, but once you do, you will be able to watch as your investments grow that sum!

How to Transition From Your Day Job to Full-Time Online Income

Once you begin to make money from your side gig, or your second source of income, you can begin to scale back the hours you spend working your day job and transition to gaining your income from this side hustle alone.

Most people who start their side hustle still have to work a traditional full-time job simultaneously. The reason for this is because side hustles may not generate enough (or any) income until you get the proper traction and marketing to begin making money. Having a full-time job enables you to have the ability to pay your bills while also spending some of your free time building your side-hustle, so eventually, it does start creating a separate stream of income.

In the beginning, you will have two sources of active income, one is your day job, and the second being the income that you make from your side hustle business. However, you could turn your side hustle business into a passive income source if you can grow it to the point where you can employ other people to work for your business or offer services to your business. At that point, you can hire somebody else to manage your business functions, such as accounting and operations, and you can sit back and just collect the money as it comes in. At this point, it will become a passive income source for you.

Getting to the point of gaining passive income does take quite a bit of time, work, dedication, and luck. Still, if you want to develop a sustainable source of passive income without many resources, you will have to grow your side hustle until it is big enough to become a standalone business. At that point, it can begin to provide you with passive income.

Starting a side hustle business is a great way for you to start saving some extra money. This extra money will open up two options for you;

- The first option is to grow your coaching business into one that is big enough that it turns into a good stream of passive income.

- The second option is to grow your side hustle business into big enough where you can employ or contract other people to do the groundwork for you. What this means is that you will aim to reach a point when your side hustle business develops a reputation that is good enough for you to have a steady stream of business (or too much business for you to handle alone). At that point, you can begin hiring employees or contractors to work for your business. Hiring people is a good way to turn your side hustle business into a passive income source. If done properly, you would be able to hire someone to manage your operations and a team of people that work with your clients while you sit back and enjoy the flow of revenue.

One thing to keep in mind is that in between, as you grow your business, there may be a period where this becomes an active income source. There may come the point while growing your side hustle business when its income begins to exceed your current active income (your day job). At this point, you can comfortably replace your day job with your side hustle (aka, your side hustle becomes your day job). However, this would mean that your coaching business will not become a stream of passive income. If, though, you choose the second option instead, you can hire others to run your business while you continue your day job.

You ideally want to upgrade your passive income as you earn more money to eventually achieve one or several short-term goals that will help you meet your specific financial freedom goals in the future. Regardless of which option you choose, one of your interim goals should be to save up the money you make from your side-hustle to eventually build a strong stream of passive income. One example of a strong investment is investing in a property, for example, as this is one of the most secure and reliable investments to make. This investment can also help you develop even more passive income by doubling it as a rental property. In my opinion, the best type of passive income is some type of investment, whether it's in stocks, bonds, or property. We will discuss this further in this book, but guaranteed income (like an investment property) is the way to go if you are not risk-averse and just want to increase your overall income.

Chapter 11: Starting your Own Business

This chapter will look at a few final examples of ways to create a profitable online business. All of the examples in this chapter can provide you with quick, easy income as long as you have customers! It will take resilience and determination, but once you get your first client, you will feel great!

Examples of Quick, Profitable Online Businesses

Below are several examples of quick, profitable online businesses that you should consider starting. Some of them use online platforms, and some of them would require you to start a business and find clients from the ground-up.

Car Rental Businesses

Using your car to make extra money is one of the quickest and most reliable sources of income in the world of side gigs. The reason for this is its huge client demand, especially in major metropolitan cities.

Doing this work comes with many benefits, like building your schedule, which adds a ton of flexibility. Additionally, the income is very steady during prime hours like before or after work, Friday evenings, and weekends.

The earning potential is also quite high in this type of side gig; drivers report making anywhere from $11 per hour to $29 per hour. Factoring in its high level of flexibility and easiness of the job, that's great money! Let's begin to look at the various ways you could make money using your car.

The first way you can make a side gig out of your car is to rent your actual vehicle. It's just what you're thinking; you are essentially acting as a car rental company but only with your vehicle.

Using a car is a great passive source of income as you don't need to do anything besides confirming your customers, and you receive money from them using your car.

Unlike ridesharing gigs like Uber and Lyft, you don't need to put in the hours to generate income actively; as long as your car is in decent shape, you can make money just by letting someone else use it temporarily. This method is a great option for making good money by renting your car out if you don't use it a lot.

Platforms such as Getaround, Turo, and Hyrecar pay you money to rent out your car just like any car rental company would, and you essentially get paid for doing nothing at all!

Average car renters make anywhere between $500 - $800 per month renting out their car. If you rent it out 100% of the month, you will make more money than only renting it 50% of the time. The car model makes a difference, so if you have a fancy car like a Tesla, you can make a premium.

Turo
At the moment, it seems like Turo is the most popular platform in terms of car rentals, so that is one platform you can look into if you are interested in renting out your car. This platform also comes with a nice feature to estimate how much your specific make and car model can make for you. This feature is ideal if you want to estimate its income before diving right into this type of side gig. With its increase in popularity throughout major cities, especially those with high tourism, you can make some serious cash by just letting someone drive your car for a few days! Not only does this help you make some extra cash if you are currently financing or leasing your car, but you can also use this money to help break-even with your purchase. Two birds, one stone!

Getaround
Getaround is a similar platform to Turo in that it offers the same services. It does not have the same feature as Turo with the estimation calculator. Still, you could consider cross-posting your car into multiple car-share websites to maximize the number of times you can rent your car by maximizing your reach. The earning potential is highly dependent on what type of car you have and the demand in your city, but most car-renters report making anywhere from $500 - $800 per month.

HyreCar

HyreCar is an interesting platform as it is a combination of Turo and Getaround mixed with Uber and Lyft. Its services are specialized towards people who don't have a car but want to pursue rideshare jobs. HyreCar allows people to rent Uber/Lyft qualified cars to use Uber and Lyft to make money. This platform is an option for you as well in terms of side gigs.

If you don't have a car, you can rent a car starting from $25 per day and generate income through rideshare or food delivery services. If you DO have a car of your own, you can make money by posting on HyreCar and renting it to someone else who wants to use it for Uber or Lyft to generate their income.

Again, if renting out your car is an option you are looking to pursue, cross-posting on these sites will help you generate the most business. Remember that renting out your car is a passive income. It allows you to do something else to make more money as a more primary and active source of money.

Starting Your Own Car Rental Business

The final option for renting your car is to create your own car rental business. If you have multiple cars that you don't mind renting out, you can create your own business. By doing it this way, you don't have to pay fees to a platform such as Turo or Getaround, but it will come with its own set of challenges. The great thing about using a platform like Turo is that the insurance for your renter is included. If you are planning on creating your own business, there will be many more logistical issues for you to look into, such as insurance, car storage, and so on. If you have ample resources at your fingertips, this could be a great option for you, but ensure that you look into everything involved before pursuing this option.

Food Delivery Businesses

Another very popular side gig these days that you can do with a car or some means of transportation is acting as a delivery service. People may need many different kinds of delivery services, but the most popular in today's world is food delivery.

Services like UberEats, Foodora, and Doordash frequently employ a team of food delivery people to pick up food from restaurants and deliver it to the person who ordered it. This type of side hustle originally started with delivering food from established restaurants but now have evolved into delivering everyday items like groceries, over the counter medicine, and alcohol.

If you own a vehicle or a bicycle and enjoy roaming through the city you live in, you can sign up and make some money doing so. The type of transportation you use will largely depend on your resources, but there is no shame in starting on a bicycle until you have enough money to buy a car. These couriers have reported that they make around $12 - $20 an hour. If you dedicate an extra 10 hours of your week to this side hustle, you can make an extra $120 - $200 per week, grossing $480 - $800 of extra monthly income. This method is not a passive source of income in any way, but it is a second active income that you can add to your earnings on your way to developing passive income.

Creating Your Own Delivery Business
If you have the means, you can create your own delivery business, which will allow you to make passive income. This delivery business could be a courier service, a food delivery service, or any other delivery service type. If you create a business like this, you can employ drivers and delivery persons, which will allow you to take a more hands-off approach and make passive income.

Dog Walking

This type of side gig is up and coming and is slowly increasing in popularity. If you live in a big metropolitan city, you likely know that most people are gone from 8 – 10 hours a day at their day job, leaving their pets with no one to look after them. This trend began the rise of dog walking in big cities. There are a few different ways that you can do this, including starting your own dog walking business or finding work through an online platform.

Companies like Rover employ contractors that love animals to help other people walk their dogs when they're not home. They also offer more passive services, like dog sitting or cat sitting, where you either take the person's pet into your own home and care for them while the owners are away, or you make drop-in visits to someone else's home to care for their pets (likely cats in this scenario).

However, when it comes to dog walking, the hours are usually during the day where other people at work. For this reason, this option wouldn't work as a side hustle if you are someone that works the regular hours of 9 – 5 (or somewhere around there).

However, you could work as a pet sitter as that requires slightly less involvement compared to dog walking. Dog walkers that do it part-time for about one week out of a month usually make around $1000, while pet sitters make around the same.

House Sitting

House sitting is a great side-gig as you can rent out your property while you are living somewhere else (and make rental income) while also getting paid for watching over someone else's home while they are away.

There are many platforms that can connect you with this kind of opportunity, like *House Sitters America* or *Trusted House Sitters,* that specialize in matching people who require house sitters to people who are interested in doing it. Another way to make money is by creating and running your own house-sitting business. You will need to find people who trust you to look after their house at the beginning, but once you build a reputation for yourself, you may find that many people want you to look after their house while they go on vacation. This is a great option if you don't mind moving from house to house, depending on where the business is.

Often, house sitting entails watering plants, bringing in mail, and keeping the person's home safe and clean throughout their trip. Although this type of side-hustle is not as popular as the ones listed prior, it is one that requires minimal effort, and you can incorporate other side-hustles (like renting out your own home while you are living at someone else's) to maximize your income.

Conclusion

As you can see, in today's world, there is an abundance of ways to make money, all you have to do is get creative, and you can find financial independence! I hope that this book has given you numerous ideas and places to turn for extra, quick money.

I challenge you to begin pursuing one or two of the side gigs in this book, and you will see for yourself how much potential there is out there!

Finally, if you like this book and recommend it to others, please leave us a positive review on Amazon! I appreciate you choosing this book, and your review would help me reach as many people as possible.

Copyright © 2021 Kenneth C. Lorenz
All rights reserved.

Made in the USA
Las Vegas, NV
06 May 2022